ASSESSMENT CENTRES

Identifying and developing competence

Charles Woodruffe

Institute of Personnel Management

Phototypeset by Paragon Photoset, Aylesbury
and printed in Great Britain by
Short Run Press, Exeter

British Library Cataloguing in Publication Data
Woodruffe, Charles
Assessment centres.
1. Management assessment centres
I. Title II. Institute of Personnel Management
658.407124

ISBN 0-85292-440-2
ISBN 0-85292-499-2 (paperback edn.).

Contents

List of Figures

Preface

This book aims to give the reader a good working knowledge of assessment centres. The main audience I hope will benefit from it are people in the human resource function. They might be managers or internal specialists who are working alongside consultants and who want to consolidate a transfer of skills from the consultants to themselves. Alternatively, they might be managers who are hoping to design a centre themselves, without the aid of a consultant. Finally, they might be the human resource (HR) managers and directors who are overseeing the organization's assessment and development activities.

The book is also aimed at line managers who want to find out about assessment centres, perhaps because they are involved in designing exercises and acting as assessors. Sections of the book certainly will be relevant to the training of assessors. Particular chapters should also be of interest to people who are more experienced in the design of assessment centres. Finally, it should be relevant to students of personnel management.

To meet the needs of the main audience, my aim is to go through the main issues and stages of assessment centre design. At this point, let me stress that I do not underplay the intricacies of assessment centre design. Nor do I want to underestimate the skill and work that is required. Indeed, I well remember the feeling when I was set to design my first centre, and my relief that I had someone with experience and expertise to advise me. At that stage, I needed this book, but it would still have been useful to have someone to talk to on the matter! Nevertheless, I do think the mysteries of assessment centres are often exaggerated. I am sure that the skills of their design can be acquired quite quickly by people blessed with common-sense.

Whilst aimed at the practitioner, I hope the book does not offend more academic colleagues. My main aim is to give straightforward and practical advice to the book's primary audience, but I have tried also to incorporate research findings and debates.

The format of the book revolves around the chronology of designing an assessment centre, and concludes with a chapter on the current controversies in assessment centre design. An appreciation of these controversies has, of course, influenced the earlier chapters.

Chapter 1 introduces assessment centres, and Chapter 2 considers their place as part of an overall HR strategy and system. Chapter 3 discusses the decision whether to have a centre, and considers the issue of gaining organizational commitment to the centre. Chapter 4 takes an overview of the assessment centre project, which is followed up in the next seven chapters. Chapter 5 describes how the competencies to be measured at the centre are determined, and Chapter 6 deals with the design of the assessment centre exercises. Chapter 7 deals with non-exercise material, and Chapter 8 considers preselection to the centre as well as briefing documents. Chapter 9 describes the various people required to run a centre, whilst Chapters 10 and 11 deal with the assessing itself together with the training of assessors. Chapter 12 discusses the follow-up to the centre, and Chapter 13 describes the process of review that should take place after a number of centres have run. Finally, Chapter 14 looks at major issues in assessment centre design, and talks about future developments in the area.

Finally, I would like to acknowledge the clients and colleagues with whom I have worked on assessment centres over the past few years, and who have taught me all that I am now passing on in this book. I would like to single out Tony Cockerill of National Westminster Bank; David Shilson, Julie Patterson and Chris Webb, plus numerous other Bank of England officials; Rob Feltham and Judith Spencer of the Civil Service Commission; Brian O'Neill of British Airways; Chrysanthi Drakou from the Bank of Cyprus; and Carol Rothwell of Rothwell Douglas Limited. I also thank Maureen Chapman, Christiane Baumann and Adele Woodruffe for their inputs to my motivation level.

1: Introducing Assessment Centres

What is an assessment centre?

It is customary for writers on assessment centres to start by pointing out respectfully that an assessment centre is not a place. Understandably, the term conjures up to the newcomer an image of a suite of rooms that is dedicated to assessment activities. This is not quite correct. The term is in fact used to refer to a method or approach. Whilst some larger organizations do have physical space dedicated to their assessment work, this is certainly not the case for many organizations.

Giving a precise definition of the assessment centre method or approach is not straightforward. The 1980s saw a great liberalizing in our thinking about assessment centres. This has made defining them quite a complex task. Indeed, the term itself has been replaced in some cases by 'development centres'. The new name gets away from some of the unfortunate associations of the traditional type of assessment centre. It was very much a one-way street. Broadly speaking, people were assessed in a rather cold and detached way by assessors who later told them what conclusions had been reached. This model might still apply to an extent for selecting outsiders to the organization. However, nowadays, for people within the organization, the focus of many centres has switched from assessment for selection to assessment for development. The change means that there is usually a much greater emphasis upon assessment being carried out collaboratively with participants, rather than something that is done to them. This new emphasis has led to some radical thinking about what should take place at the centre. In some cases, it might not be necessary to have assessors at all. People can assess themselves and each other to gain the insights that are required to plan out their development.

The definition of an assessment centre must capture the common denominator amidst this diversity. A starting point is to recognize that there is a common objective, and this is the 'assessment' part of the title. All centres aim to give information about the participants' current or potential competence. This objective is true whether the centre is for selection or development. It might be competence to fulfil a particular job or it might be competence to succeed at a level of work (eg middle management) within the organization. In turn, the purpose of making this assessment of competence is to ensure, by a combination of selection and development, that the organization has the human resources it needs.

So one defining characteristic of assessment centres is their objective: to obtain the best possible indication of people's actual or potential competence to perform at the target job or job level. The assessment centre approach or method of achieving this objective is to combine a range of assessment techniques so that the fullest and clearest indication of competence is achieved. These techniques will include exercises that get participants to carry out simulations of the work of the target job or job level. Performance in the simulation is measured in terms of the same competency dimensions that are important for the target job. The logic is straightforward. If the objective is to find out people's competence to perform a job, the surest route is to capture the essence of the job in a set of simulations. People's performance at the simulations should be predictive of their behaviour in the job itself.

Assessment centres therefore focus squarely upon behaviour and include a set of exercises to capture and simulate the major aspects of the job. A simplified example is a job that involves desk-work, meetings with individuals and meetings in groups. The assessment centre for that job might include an in-tray and an analytical exercise (to simulate the desk-work), a meeting with a customer or subordinate (played by a role player and simulating the meetings with individuals) and a group negotiation or problem-solving meeting (to reflect the meetings in groups). It can be seen that there are two broad classes of exercise, namely written and interactive (the one-to-one role plays and the group exercises). The variety of these simulation exercises is important: Gaugler *et al* (1987) found that centres were more valid predictors when a greater range of exercises was used.

Beyond the common objective and the inclusion of simulations, there are few hard and fast rules. Indeed, one of the advantages of the assessment centre method is that it is flexible: the centre should be designed to meet the needs of the organization, be they development, selection or some combination of the two. This might mean that the centre includes one or more interviews, as well as psychological tests, self-assessment and peer-assessment. On the other hand, it might only consist of the simulations. Similarly, it might include participants giving consideration to their career aspirations, and being given help with planning their development. However, these should only be part of the centre if they help to fulfil its purposes.

Indeed, the whole centre will be designed to be congruent with its end purpose. For example, if the objective is people's development, it is crucial to design a centre that will marry the need for an assessment that is technically accurate with the requirement for participants to have an experience that is developmental. Practical constraints must also be kept in mind. There is no point in designing a brilliantly accurate graduate assessment centre that lasts a week.

In short, an assessment centre must combine the technical objective of accurate assessment with the consultancy objective of acceptability and ownership. Technical accuracy on the one hand, and acceptability on the other, are the twin yardsticks by which practical assessment procedures are judged. There will be circumstances, especially with centres for development, in which the need for acceptability will outweigh the need for technical accuracy.

Features of assessment centres

Whilst it is important to think freely and creatively in the design of a centre, there are a number of generalizations that can be made about the typical centre. First of all, several people participate in the centre at the same time. Six is the usual number in each batch of people, but there might be more than one batch running in parallel. The people in each batch take part together in the group exercises, and complete the other exercises on their own. Having people participate in batches makes group exercises easy to carry out, reduces the unit cost of the centre, and makes for a lighter approach than the individual assessment procedure of seeing people one at a time. However, like all the generalizations, it is not a defining requirement. If there were insufficient numbers of participants or very senior people were being assessed, they might be seen one at a time, perhaps using role players for any group exercises.

The second generalization is that people are observed by a team of assessors. A ratio that works well is one assessor for each pair of participants, so that each participant is assessed during the centre by three assessors. Again, the rule can be broken. A more developmental centre might rely entirely on self-assessment and peer-assessment. Whoever the assessors are, however, they will need to be trained thoroughly in the competency dimensions that they are meant to be assessing.

Assessment is by a combination of methods, which means that it is unlikely that an assessment centre will last less than four hours. With internal centres, the assessment can last two to three days, and the developmental component will then add further to this time.

All the information from the assessment techniques will be brought together, and usually this is done under the headings of the competencies that are crucial for high performance in the job. The alternative procedure is to gather the information under the headings of the simulation exercises that represent the various aspects of the job.

The competencies are behavioural dimensions. They frequently have as titles the traits or dispositions that could be used to 'explain' people's behaviour. The two broad classes of competency identified by Russell (1985) are problem solving (eg analysis, breadth of awareness) and interpersonal (eg sensitivity, self-confidence).

The growth of assessment centres

A brief history

There is nothing new about assessment centres. Their history in the United Kingdom dates back to the War Office Selection Boards (WOSB), which were introduced in 1942 to select officers. Anstey (1989) recounts that the system the Boards replaced had clearly broken down: a high percentage of people it passed had to be 'returned to unit' because of their lack of ability. The old system relied on interviewing people who had been judged as likely to be of officer quality. The judgement was from their background or from their achievements in the ranks. These achievements could range from gallantry to exceptional smartness. With this method of preselection, the old system missed the chance of interviewing many people who actually had officer potential. Furthermore, it incorrectly ascribed potential to large numbers of those it did get to assess.

The new system was devised by the Directorate for the Selection of Personnel and included leaderless group exercises, objective selection tests, and separate personal interviews by three assessors. The assessors were a senior and a junior officer and a psychiatrist. Anstey describes how the new procedure resulted in a 'dramatic drop' in the percentage of people returned to unit. Its success led to its acceptance throughout the Army.

In the United States, the pioneering work was undertaken by the

Office of Strategic Studies, which used the method to select spies during the Second World War, (MacKinnon, 1977). This early United States assessment centre was also derived from the War Office Selection Boards, but after the war the United Kingdom and United States approaches diverged somewhat, (Feltham, 1988a).

In the United Kingdom, assessment centres were developed in peacetime by the Civil Service and other parts of the public sector. They followed the model of the WOSB, and were sometimes labelled extended interviews. In the United States, postwar development moved to the private sector. The pioneer was the American Telephone and Telegraph Company (AT&T), which used assessment centres in its Management Progress Study, which began in 1956 (Bray, 1964). The method was taken up by Standard Oil of Ohio in 1962, and then by IBM, Sears, General Electric and J C Penney (Finkle, 1976).

As Feltham (1988a) notes, the United Kingdom and United States traditions have definite differences. In particular, the British public-sector model relies more upon interviews than the American private-sector model. Indeed, the British public-sector assessment centre is sometimes called an extended interview. Other differences detailed by Feltham are the British emphasis upon group exercises with an assigned leader, practical/physical group exercises, unstructured group discussions and fairly long written exercises. On the other hand, American assessment centres place more emphasis on in-tray exercises, group exercises without a leader but with assigned roles, and two-person role plays.

Assessment centres in use today in the United Kingdom private sector probably owe more in direct terms to the developments in the United States and to the American assessment model than to the British public-sector model. However, some of the centres in the British private sector are modelled upon the old public-sector format, just as there are now some centres in the UK public sector that are in line with the private sector and the American tradition.

Current usage

The use of assessment centres in the United States is widespread, and in the United Kingdom it has grown rapidly in the 1980s. In the United States, Gaugler *et al* (1987) estimate that in the mid-1980s over 2,000 American organizations were using some type of assessment centre programme. In the United Kingdom, a survey in 1989 (Mabey, 1989) found that over a third of companies employing more than 1,000 people had used an assessment centre in the past year. A less formal survey in the same year covering a greater range of companies found that just under 20 per cent of respondents' organizations used assessment centres (Curnow, 1989). A few years earlier, Robertson and Makin (1986) found that just over a quarter of UK organizations employing more than 500 people used assessment centres. They also found that the usage depended upon the volume of people the organization recruited. Just over a third of large recruiters of managers used them, compared with a tenth of the minor recruiters.

Although the use of assessment centres is becoming widespread, in many of these organizations it is likely to be patchy (eg just for selecting graduates). For example, Robertson and Makin (1986) found that 75 per cent of the large recruiters using assessment centres used them for less than half their managerial applicants.

The seductiveness of assessment centres

The use of assessment centres has increased despite the cost of their installation and the on-going cost of operating them. The typical centre will take three managers away from their jobs to act as assessors for one to five days. If used with current employees it will also take them from their jobs. In addition, there is the need for administrative back-up, and in many cases the hire of suitable accommodation.

One reason that all this investment is seen as worthwhile is the belief in the quality of the assessment that is obtained. Accurate assessment is crucial in selecting people both for jobs and for career paths. It is also highly desirable for identifying people's development programmes. The assessment centre process has extreme credibility in terms of delivering accurate assessment. The belief in assessment centres is partly the result of a good deal of research evidence in their favour. This research evidence is translated quite readily into the message that they have been proved to be virtually 100 per cent accurate. In fact, there are a number of questions raised about assessment centres in the more academic journals, and there are published instances of them not working. These issues are dealt with in Chapter 14. However, the fact is that these question marks have had little impact on the end users of assessment centres.

Aside from the headline summary of the research evidence, people believe in assessment centres because of the persuasive logic of their design. The centres sample the participants' behaviour in a set of simulations of the target job. Participants are assessed against the dimensions of performance for that job, and these competency dimensions will be clearly visible in the simulations. Furthermore, there is the double-check that if the competency dimensions are not clearly visible in people's performance of the simulations, then either the dimensions or the simulations are wrong. The rationality of the centres is extended by having assessors who are well trained in the observation, recording, classifying and rating of behaviour. The logical foundation of assessment centres was cited as a benefit by assessment centre users in a range of different countries when they were questioned by Imada *et al* (1985). These users saw the centre as a better tool for making decisions, and therefore it is also seen as a fairer approach.

Aside from the assessment centre's logic and accuracy, its other obvious selling point is the impetus it gives to a management development programme. The centre will provide a clear and energized starting point to the development process. A well-conducted assessment centre is the best way of getting people to buy into and take responsibility for their own development plan. The planning will be based around behaviour that definitely took place during the exercises, and the priorities for development will be apparent. If the exercises are tailor made, the areas of strength and weakness will have been identified within settings that belong to the organization. This makes the feedback particularly persuasive. People can see that if they are to succeed within the organization they must develop. In addition to the feedback on performance in the exercises, there can be other developmental aspects to the centre. For example, it might emphasize self-assessment and the diagnosis by participants of their own and each other's strengths and limitations during the centre. It might also include consideration by participants of their career aspirations and possibilities.

This discussion on the seductiveness of assessment centres can be summarized by saying that assessment centres sell themselves. An optimistic headline summary of the literature, coupled with their intuitive appeal, means that they enjoy the support of both assessors and participants. The assessors see how people behave in the centre and can be confident that this is a good indication of how they would behave in the job. In addition, if the centres are used for selection, participants come through the centre feeling that the organization has treated them fairly and that it has obtained sound evidence for its decision. They will also have enjoyed a preview of work within the organization, which will give them a firm basis for deciding about any eventual offer of employment. If the centres are used for development, participants will gain valuable insights from their own experience of the centre and from the feedback by assessors and possibly peers. As Strube *et al* (1986) have demonstrated, the need for accurate self-appraisal outweighs the need for self-enhancement, and centres undoubtedly appear to satisfy the former need if not the latter.

In fact, all this faith is only likely to be well founded if the centre has been carefully and rigorously designed, and if checks are kept on its operation. Unfortunately, there are plenty of examples of assessment centres with exercises that are poorly designed, and that have little bearing on the target job; where information is gathered unsystematically and without its relevance being made explicit; where assessors are poorly trained; and where participants are alienated from the procedure. Yet the operators will often still keep faith even with the poorest centre, probably because of their personal investment in its design.

Behind the growth

The fundamental reason for the escalating demand for assessment centres is that the need for assessment has increased. Assessment centres are seen as the best answer to this need.

One aspect of the growing need for accurate assessment is that organizations are having to be more certain in choosing between applicants. Mistakes are ever more expensive. The mistake might be in accepting people who are not suitable, but nowadays the more important mistake for many organizations is in rejecting people who could have made a valuable contribution. In an era of shortages of talent and experience, it is critical to recognize people who could contribute to the organization's success. Furthermore, the way the organization selects people must help it sell itself to potential recruits.

A related and increasingly important aspect of the need for assessment is that it allows the organization to place its new recruits wisely according to their strengths and interests. The organization can make the best use of applicants' talent and, in the longer term, this will help to maintain people's commitment and motivation.

For people already in the organization, assessment centres facilitate a joint approach in which the organization and participants collaborate to make career plans and to arrive at development plans. The centres contribute to fostering and realizing people's talent and to motivating people through their development.

The importance of recognizing and developing talent should be seen against the need for organizations to have the highest quality of human resources. They need people who can enable them to respond to the challenges they face. The turbulent environment written about by Emery and Trist (1965) a quarter of a century ago has come of age. Organizations must be responsive in an uncertain world. They need to identify those people most suited to join their pools of talent, and they must also identify and meet these people's development needs.

Change and complexity has also resulted in the specification for the successful manager itself becoming more exacting. People are required who are adaptable and tolerant of the ambiguity of change. They need both a high level of cognitive skills and strong interpersonal abilities. Couple these demands with demographic shortages, and it is apparent that organizations simply cannot afford to waste the talents of the people available to them. For example, Skapinker (1989b) reports how Triplex Lloyd set up a one-day assessment centre to help identify managerial talent amongst its shop-floor staff. The programme was a result of the Chief Executive's enlightened belief that many of these staff were more talented than their immediate superiors realized.

The supply side

The discussion so far has been on the demand side of the growth story. It should be added that the demand for assessment centres has been matched by supply. There is an increasing number of consultants in the area. Indeed, consultants have played an educational role and have therefore to some extent fuelled the demand.

The side benefits

The growth of assessment centres can largely be attributed to their obvious uses in selecting people and helping to place and develop them. However there is also a set of beneficial side effects.

Assessor benefits

The process of being trained as an assessor carries the general benefit of imparting the skills of assessing people and of giving feedback. These skills will be useful in the assessor's normal job of managing people (Glaze, 1989).

Assessors also benefit simply from being part of an assessor team. People from different parts of the organization work together and build a network. Being chosen as an assessor can also give the person a feeling of the confidence the organization has in him or her. Assessors are being entrusted with a highly responsible task. Confidence is further built up by the process of having to present an opinion on participants regularly at assessors' conferences.

Analysis of competencies
The disciplined approach to assessment forces the organization to analyse its jobs properly. It also results in the common language of the competency dimensions that differentiate the successful from the average performer. Through assessor training these dimensions can become part of the folklore of the organization. As Glaze (1989) says, commenting upon the experience of Cadbury Schweppes, competencies become 'absorbed in the bloodstream of the organization' (p 44). One organization that I worked with had a list of 12 competencies that became well known as the 12 c's, and were thoroughly internalized throughout the organization. It even reached the point of a yuletide humourist producing the 12 incompetencies, which he saw as a better representation of reality.

Of course a thorough job analysis can be carried out quite independently of any decision about having an assessment centre. However, the design of an assessment centre requires that a thorough analysis is carried out, and so acts as a real impetus.

Performance appraisal
The competencies can become part of an appraisal system. This will contribute to a rational and integrated overall system of human resource assessment and development, and will specifically improve the appraisal process because the competencies will be well understood. The appraisal system will also benefit from line managers who are assessors being better able to carry out appraisal interviews and to give specific behavioural examples to substantiate their judgements on performance.

Recruitment
Assessment centres can also be used to sell the organization. Candidates see them as a sign that the organization is thoroughly professional in its personnel practices. Successful applicants will also be subject to the psychological effect of feeling committed to an organization that puts them through a rigorous selection process before letting them in (Fletcher, 1989).

Applicants also get a taste for the job. The centre should be realistic, but in the process it might well draw people's attention to the more positive aspects of the job. A realistic preview boosts people's overall opinion of the organization. Meglino *et al* (1988) demonstrated the beneficial effects of a realistic job preview on trainees' turnover and on their perception of the organization as caring, trustworthy and honest. It should also show people who really are not suited to the work their lack of compatibility with it. The preview should thereby help to cut early turnover from unwise choices.

Of course, if a well designed centre has a recruitment advantage, by the same token, a badly designed and administered centre can lose potential recruits.

Motivation

Participants at internal centres can gain a sense of being valued by the organization through being chosen to attend the centre. Attendance implies a vote of confidence and is a clear sign of the organization devoting resources to their development. If the centre is well designed and developmental, participants should go away remotivated. Again, the sting in the tail is that if it is badly designed, they will depart demotivated.

2: Assessment Centres and the Human Resource System

The link with organizational strategy

Assessment centres should be part of a human resource strategy to ensure that the organization can meet its strategic objectives by having competent people. The centres are integral to career path planning and development. The overall aim is that the organization has people ready and willing to perform its jobs to a high level of competence. Equally, people themselves will gain by participating in the planning of a career that matches their aspirations and strengths. In short, there should be a better fit or match between what the organization and its employees need and have to offer each other (Schein, 1978).

From the organization's point of view, the centre provides an audit of people's competencies. It might well also include exercises to get people to think about their interests and aspirations. The organization can then plan to match people's competencies and interests with the known requirements and features of jobs or job levels.

It might seek to ensure that it has people with the competencies required for its jobs by selection, development, or – more likely – a combination of the two. If the assessment centre is used purely for selection, the organization can choose people who come closest to matching its requirements, and place them in the jobs to which they are most suited, and which match their interests. On the other hand, when it is used for development, the centre will sensitize people to their strengths and development needs, and can be used as the starting point for a management development programme. The overall aim is to help people to do their present jobs better and to choose future jobs and develop competence for them.

In simple terms, then, the flow starts with the organization deciding its mission and strategy. This leads to a decision on how it should be structured, and what jobs therefore exist. The requirements for successful performance in each job can then be specified, and the assessment procedure is designed to measure people's competence to perform those jobs. At the same time, the development system must be installed to help people increase their competence. This flow is represented in Figure 1 below.

Figure 1
Linking HR processes to organizational strategy

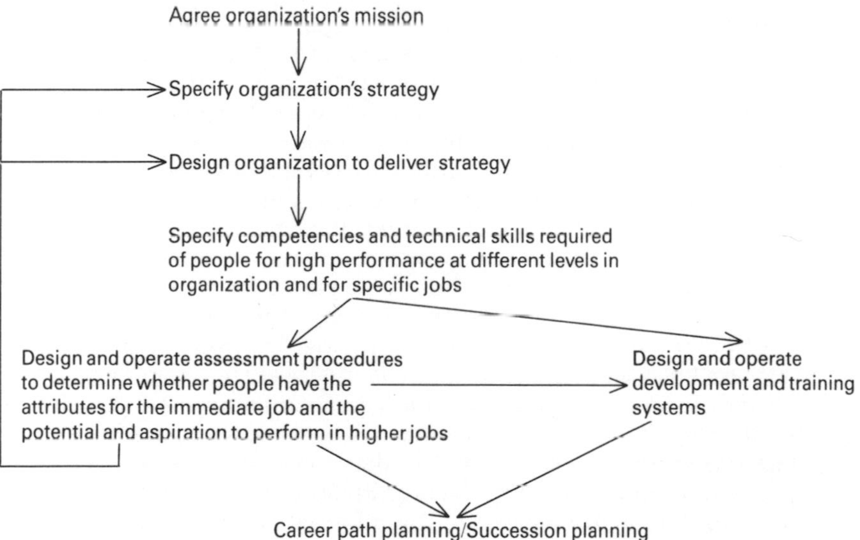

An example is provided by a financial services organization with whom I worked, whose mission was to be the dominant market leader. This was to be fulfilled by being a high-quality customer-driven and sales-oriented organization. I worked with them to specify the requirements they had of people, in terms of the competencies that were needed at different levels in the organization. We designed an assessment process to audit present and prospective staff against these competencies as well as introducing development and training procedures targeted upon the same competencies.

As Figure 1 shows, information from the operation of assessment centres should feed back into strategy and organizational design. For example, it might be found that the necessary human resources are not available within the organization or externally to match its requirements, given its growth targets etc. If this is the case, the organization must change its needs by redesign or by a change of strategy. The growth plans themselves might need to be reviewed, and so the assessment centre will have had an influence upon strategy and will not just be the implementation of strategy. Less dramatically, the assessment process will feed back into priorities for training provision. With the organization referred to above, the assessment process found that existing branch staff were very weak at marketing and sales. It might have been decided to reorganize and have specialist sales officers. In fact an urgent programme of training was carried out.

It is important that the context of assessment centres is thought through in this way. Otherwise all the benefits of the process will not be gained. For example, some organizations have assessment centres for graduate selection, but seem to think of them purely as a way of choosing from amongst applicants. They do not make the maximum use of the information from the centre to lay down the successful applicants' initial development plans. Other organizations have internal centres to which people go purely for the organization to make immediate choices about them. The choice might be whether they should be promoted or go on a fast-track programme. This non-integrated type of centre frequently assesses people against a particular list of competencies which are found nowhere else in the human resource system. The centres are not seen as a rich source of information that should be used to determine development plans, and most importantly to help the organization plan its future knowing the resources it has available. The information could be used to anticipate future gluts or shortfalls of staff, and be the basis of a thorough process of succession and career planning.

Gratton and Syrett (1990) point out how different succession strategies are adopted by different organizations to suit their circumstances. For example, IBM grooms people for years, having identified their talent early on via assessment centres, whereas Amstrad relies on shorter-term 'fixes'. BAT leaves succession largely to its constituent companies but negotiates moves between companies for the most able, whilst Hanson operates purely as a holding company. The major difference between these companies is not so much the principle of having a succession strategy, as determining what people are going to succeed to. In the case of IBM actual posts can be identified. In the case of Amstrad the future is far less certain.

What they need to specify is the qualities of the flexible manager, and to audit their present people so that obvious shortfalls can be identified. Indeed, had Amstrad done this, they would possibly have avoided problems they encountered when they decided to take a more central role in production (Fonda, 1989).

The type of organization represented by Amstrad is increasingly the organization of the future. The turbulent environment with its unremitting change means that long-range succession planning for particular posts will be less and less possible. The emphasis will be upon identifying potential to move to levels of responsibility, and developing people accordingly. Just such a process has been described by Stamp (1989) under the title 'career path appreciation'. Whilst her methodology is different from the assessment centre approach, the fundamental concept could be used in the assessment centre and succession planning context. Her concept is that there are particular levels of work within organizations. Under the assessment centre approach, these levels would be associated with particular sets of competencies. The level that people have attained and the level they could attain would be measured by the assessment centre, and the development system would bridge the gap. In addition, the centre would help people examine the level they want to attain.

Whilst long term succession planning will increasingly be about people's ability and wish to succeed to levels of responsibility, the model of short-term succession to particular jobs also needs to be more sophisticated than it often is at present. The jobs themselves will change at short notice as the organization changes, and Gratton and Syrett (1990) point out that the reality is that jobs are moulded around people just as much as people are developed for jobs. For example, a person might want to retain a scientific or professional role as well as taking on managerial responsibility. The need for information about people's wishes can be accommodated in the assessment centre design by including, for example, a measure of people's career anchors (Schein, 1978).

In summary, the succession planning process is a far more complex and iterative procedure than in the days of predictability. It must be fitted to the current realities facing the organization, a focus that must be shared by the whole HR system. Nowadays, the reality is change and uncertainty and the need to be responsive. This must be reflected in systems of assessment and development. The assessment must be against the competency dimensions of change rather than of stasis, and the development systems must equip people for longer-term change, whilst also being responsive to their development needs in the shorter term. Sometimes the assessment centre will examine people against specific jobs. Increasingly, however, the focus will be to help people prepare for a future level (eg to join a flexible pool of senior managers), and for the change inherent in the particular jobs they might assume.

The assessment and development system

Assessment centres must be integrated within an overall HR assessment and development system so that the end result is a highly rational, coherent and integrated system of HR management. An example of such a system is the model in Figure 2. There is a selection centre for graduate intake, which has a pass/fail emphasis, though it is backed by a management development system for the successful. For internal staff, there are centres that are more developmental at the doorways to junior, middle, and senior management. Each centre is backed up by a system of management development workshops and modules. So each internal centre identifies people's strengths as well as areas upon which they should focus for development. The management development system then takes over, to round up people's strengths, and to work on their development needs. It will also prepare people who are provisionally seen as joining the pool of senior management talent. Thus assessment centres are bound in with management development in meeting the organization's HR needs. The assessment centres give an accurate indication of people's competencies and provide an impetus to the management development programme.

Figure 2 on page 18 shows in detail how the centres are positioned within the human resource development system. The internal centres come after some management development has taken place as well as being the gateway to further development. Competencies that can be developed easily to a person's level of potential are assessed after some developmental effort has been made. Weaknesses identified at the centre are therefore not merely superficial. This positioning will ensure that the centre is not measuring a simple deficit, which certainly should not intrude on an audit of potential. The only centre at which such deficits might be measured is one that is looking at current readiness to perform the target job.

Locating the assessment centres within an overall model of the HR development system ensures consideration of the major policy questions about what will happen after the centre. For example, if the centre is to make the decision about promotion, can people come back a second time? Does there need to be anything other than the passage of time before they return to the same centre? Is the centre the only input to the promotion decision? Questions such as these need to be considered and answered if there is to be a coherence to the system.

Assessment centre uses and designs

The precise use of the centre will dictate its design. The types of centre range from the traditional selection assessment centre through to a self-assessment centre for development. However, the distinctions of design are becoming less clear-cut because the uses are becoming blurred. In particular, selection centres increasingly contain elements of career planning and development, rather than only concerning themselves with assessment.

Centres for development

A developmental goal has become the emphasis for many internal assessment centres. One major reason for the change of emphasis of internal centres is the demotivating effects if they are used purely for selection. Conversely, there is the motivating effect of being developed. A case study of just such a change of emphasis is provided by Neill's (1989) description of Trent Regional Health Authority's fast-track management development programme. It changed from being based upon a selection centre to being a much more developmental and collaborative event.

A second reason for the change of emphasis is the realization that organizations must develop their people continuously (Wood, 1988). As described earlier, the 1980s saw the environment in which organizations operate become more and more turbulent and changeable. This fact alone meant that organizations had to emphasize the development of their human resources to meet the ever-changing demands. In addition, these demands have themselves become more exacting at the very time that demographic and societal changes have reduced the supply of people. In all, organizations have had to place an increasing emphasis upon developing available resources rather than just being able to pick from a mass of external and internal talent.

A centre for development still involves assessment of competencies. However, the end result is that participants gain an awareness of

Figure 2

Example of an integrated assessment/development process

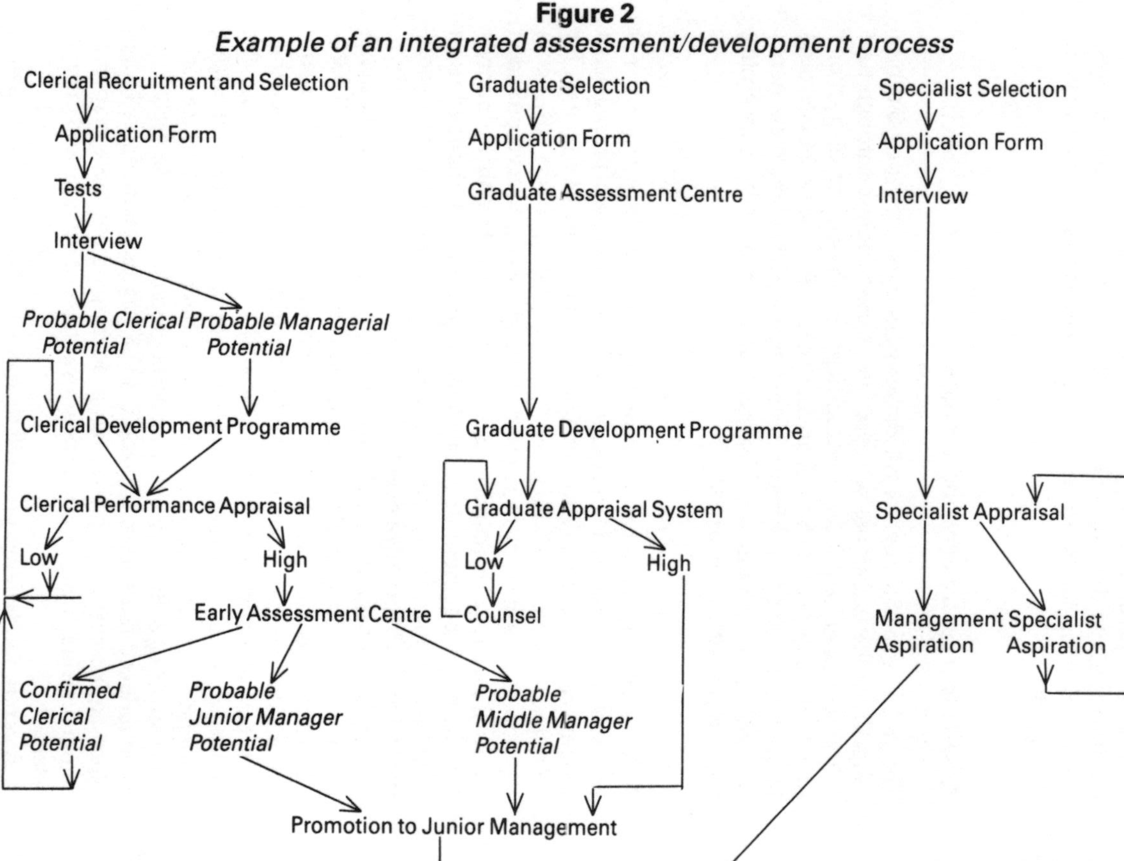

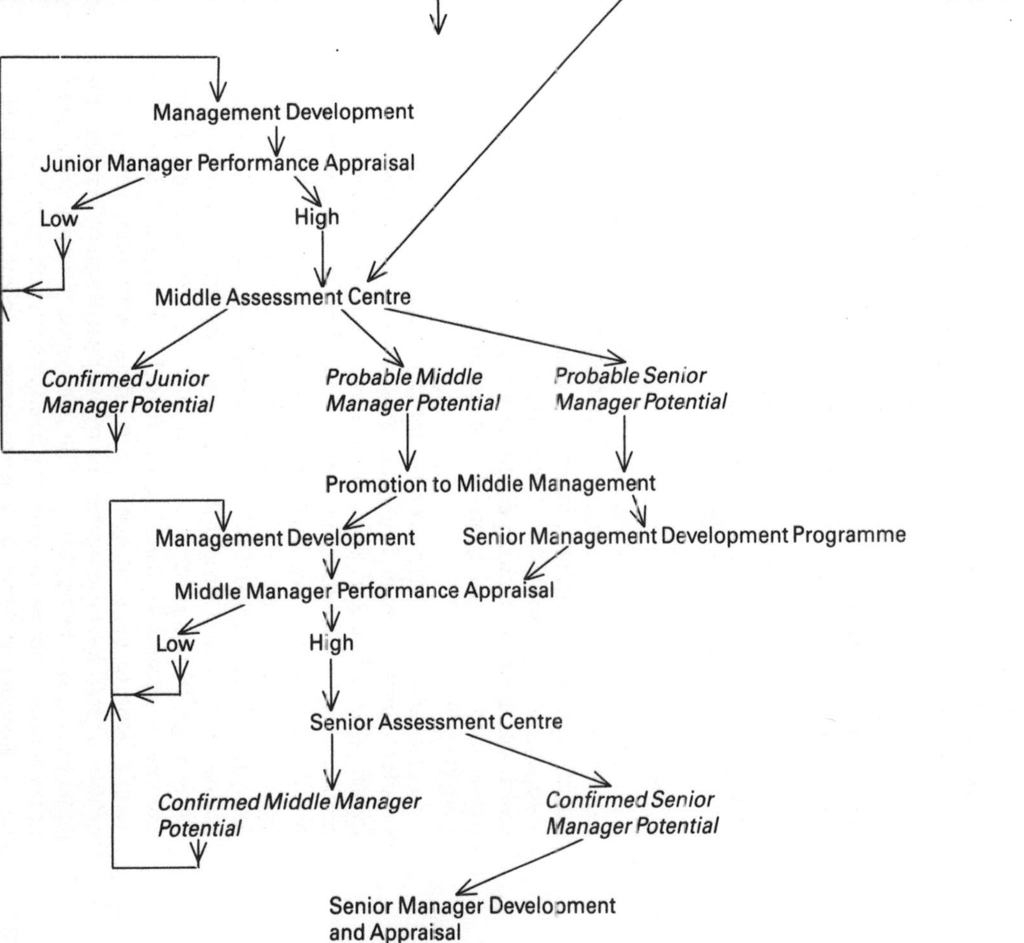
Management Development
Junior Manager Performance Appraisal
Low
High
Middle Assessment Centre
Confirmed Junior Manager Potential
Probable Middle Manager Potential
Probable Senior Manager Potential
Promotion to Middle Management
Management Development
Senior Management Development Programme
Middle Manager Performance Appraisal
Low
High
Senior Assessment Centre
Confirmed Middle Manager Potential
Confirmed Senior Manager Potential
Senior Manager Development and Appraisal

their development needs and will probably start to construct a development plan during the centre. Indeed they might well use the centre for immediate development. For example, they can have feedback and coaching after each exercise, which they can use in subsequent exercises (Griffiths and Allen, 1987). If a centre is truly for development this can have an enormously liberating effect on its design and operation. Participants can behave quite naturally and declare and discuss openly their development needs. Furthermore the centre's administrator need worry no longer about the secrecy of exercises. It might not be necessary even to have assessors. People can assess themselves and each other. For example Stevens (1985) reports on a centre which consists only of the participants and administrators. The exercises are videotaped and participants can perform their own diagnoses. Most radical of all, it might not matter so much if the assessments are accurate. The key requirement is to give a boost to the drive for development, and to get people to arrive at a development plan of their own.

Centres for selection

Assessment centres for selection can be divided into those used for external recruitment and those used for internal selection. A frequently cited example of the former is a graduate assessment centre. Two contrasting examples of internal selection centres are those which are used to identify people for a fast management track and those used for the selection of first-line managers from amongst clerical staff.

At first sight, assessment centres for external selection might seem simpler to implement and run than those for internal selection or for development. External selection centres carry with them a less obvious need for feedback to participants. There is also less anxiety about the demotivating effects of poor performance at the centre upon those who take part. However, nowadays, even centres used for external selection should provide some feedback to participants so that they do not simply feel processed by the organization. As Herriot (1988) has pointed out, it is vital that organizations do not alienate applicants by making them feel the selection process is simply done to them. It needs to be done *with* them, and so the centres should become events for mutual assessment between the organization and its applicants. The alternative is to risk creating an unfavourable impression with applicants which will be passed on to their colleagues and friends. In turn, these people will be less willing to apply to the organization. The grapevine operates most obviously with undergraduates, with whom some organizations clearly have a much more favourable image than others because of their selection procedures.

The demographic changes that have brought about the shortage of people are having a further influence: for many organizations selection centres are moving from an accept/reject choice to the position of trying to make the best use of those people who apply to the organization. By providing so much good information on people, the assessment centre can be used not just to select, but also to place people, and to work out initial induction and development plans for them. Indeed with the shortages facing organizations, selection centres could be renamed placement centres. A client of mine who was facing difficulties attracting sufficient experienced applicants is now using an assessment centre which includes a career counselling interview. Wherever possible, a fit is achieved between this client's needs and the applicant's interests. Of course, some people will still be deemed unsuitable generally for the organization, but the tenor of the centre is clearly different from one which is exclusively for selecting people.

Assessment centres used for internal selection will definitely need to have a major emphasis on feedback and development planning. For example, Greatrex and Phillips (1989) describe how BP now stress that their residential assessment boards are a developmental opportunity for the individual, with full feedback and counselling.

Generally, it is unwise for an internal centre to be seen as an irrevocable decision-point in a person's career. Assessment centres that are set up in this way build resentment and lose their development possibilities. For example, some organizations have centres at which attendance is compulsory, and which are used for promotion, performance review, and reward. This type of centre will become an object of fear, and those who have performed less satisfactorily will feel thoroughly demotivated. I believe that it is much better if the centre is used to provide information upon people's current competence and likely potential, but to leave plenty of room for flexibility in the organization's view of them. The centre should be used to pencil their potential into the organization's succession plan, and not to make hard and fast pronouncements. My preference is also to separate the centre from an immediate promotion decision, but if it has to be used to help make immediate decisions about promotion, the participants must be debriefed extremely carefully after the centre. Ideally those who are not seen as ready for promotion will share this perception. Quite definitely, the macho approach to passing and failing internal candidates has highly dysfunctional consequences, and ones which very few organizations can afford to play down.

This does not mean abandoning any notion of some people being better than others, and identifying them. There are clearly advantages of identifying fast-track people. Boehm (1985) describes the benefits of these early-identification programmes as enabling management development resources to be focused on the individuals likely to contribute most to the organization. They also keep high-potential people motivated, and give others an honest account of where they stand so that they can make informed choices about their own future. However, as Boehm also notes, it is crucial that all those not seen as high flyers remain motivated to perform and develop at their own pace. The risk is that the organization's top 10 per cent of young managers go to the centre; 15 per cent of these are picked for the fast track; and the remaining 85 per cent of the top 10 per cent are left feeling they have failed. This sad and perverse effect is seen in all too many organizations at present. I believe that one way round it is to demonstrate that the organization's views on people's potential are not static; another is to try to make the view at any particular time one that is shared by the person involved. What must be avoided is the assessment centre that is followed up by the 'Private and Confidential' letter, telling people their worth. Indeed, I do not believe that it is necessary to motivate people by having a highly visible fast-track labelling scheme which people either manage or fail to get onto. The benefits of identifying potential cited by Boehm can still be gained with a more fluid and tentative approach that is set in the context of development.

It can be seen, then, that the distinction between using assessment centres for selection or development is breaking down. A well-designed and implemented assessment centre that is used primarily for selection will have many of the features of a centre used for development. Of course, there will be differences in follow-up, and there will be some major differences in design. For example, a developmental centre might well make more use of self-assessments, whereas this will be unrealistic in a selection centre. After all, people cannot be relied upon to vote themselves out of a job, even if it would be wise for them to do so. However, in all cases, a good centre should be a collaborative endeavour between the participants and the organization. It is something done with them, so that both the organization and its applicants or staff can reach rational, well-informed decisions about careers. Otherwise, participants are likely to go away feeling processed.

A continuum of assessment centres

So the distinctions between the ways in which assessment centres should be used and designed are becoming blurred. Nevertheless, it is possible to draw up a continuum of assessment centres as they exist, which range from the archetypical selection centre to the archetypical development centre. The continuum is summarized in Figure 3.

Figure 3

A continuum of assessment centres

	←		→
Purpose	development/career planning	promotion/development	selection
Label	development centre		selection centre
Philosophy	done by the participant	done with the participant	done to the candidate
Method	self-assessment/peer assessment plus assessor's view	assessment with feedback	testing/no feedback
Assessor's role	facilitator		judge
Includes	self-insight materials		cognitive test
Output	personal development plan	report	selection decision
Information on exercises	open		secret
Feedback given	after each exercise	after centre	not given
Owner of information	participant	participant and organization	organization
Duration	one week		one day

3: Deciding to Have an Assessment Centre

This chapter considers the published evidence for the validity of assessment centres. It also describes the economic case that can be made for them with the aid of a technique called utility analysis. Finally, it considers the arguments against their introduction.

Analytical evidence of validity

The validity of an assessment centre is broadly defined as how well the centre does what it is meant to do. Depending upon the centre's purpose, the issue might be whether it is valid as a way of choosing high performing people or whether it works as a catalyst for development. The evidence that has been published on validity concentrates on the traditional type of centre which is used for selection. The published evidence is not on the newer-style centres which are used as catalysts to development.

The indices against which selection centres have been validated are many and varied, but they fall into the two main categories of current performance in the job and performance over time in a career. For some jobs, current performance might be readily quantifiable. For example, salespeople can be measured in terms of performance against targets. However, for many jobs the criterion is less clear cut, and ratings of performance by a superior against the job competencies have to be relied upon. The second criterion is performance over time. This is frequently measured in terms of rated potential by supervisors, and so it is really dealing with anticipated performance. However, sometimes performance over time is measured in terms of realized potential via promotion or salary.

The studies on validity could be taken one by one. However, there will inevitably be variations between them, and some of the evidence will be negative. For example, Pynes and Bernardin (1989) report a correlation of 0.22 between assessment centre ratings for American police officer entrants and their subsequent job performance. They conclude that 'the results do not justify the high cost of this particular assessment center' (p 833). One reaction to these fluctuations is that the positive evidence at least shows what can be achieved with a well designed centre. Negative evidence might just cast doubt on the particular centre upon which the evidence was obtained, or might be suspect in some other way. It does not undermine the assessment centre approach. For example, Pynes and Bernardin admit that their measure of performance suffered from the fact that most ratings were near the middle of the scale, and their assessment centre ratings had the problem of being on only a three-point scale with 55 per cent of people gaining a 3. In such circumstances, a high correlation between assessment centre scores and performance would be hard to obtain.

A second reaction to fluctuating evidence is to take an overview of the validities of a number of individual assessment centres, and to find out how valid assessment centres are in general. This is the approach taken by the advocates of a methodology known as meta-analysis. It is an approach championed by Hunter *et al* (1982). The variations in validity between individual assessment centres are put down to the different errors and quirks that will always be present in different studies.

A number of meta-analyses have now been published which either deal exclusively with assessment centres or compare assessment centres with other methods of prediction. Schmitt *et al* (1984) carried out a comparative study. They surveyed validity studies published in *Personnel Psychology* and the *Journal of Applied Psychology*. They found 21 validity coefficients on assessment centres, which had been used to predict a range of criteria including ratings of people's performance and status change. Assessment centres were superior to all other methods of predicting performance ratings, with a mean coefficient of 0.43. They were also amongst the best predictors of status change with a mean coefficient of 0.41. Taking all the criteria together, Schmitt *et al* report that assessment centres were the most valid predictors (the mean validity coefficient was 0.41), along with evaluations by peers and supervisors. Personality measures were the worst predictors, with a mean validity of 0.15.

Similar statistics for assessment centres came from a study by Gaugler *et al* (1987), in which they carried out a meta-analysis of 50 validation studies of assessment centres containing a total of 107 validity coefficients. The overall validity coefficient was 0.37, the best coefficient being obtained when the centres were to predict ratings of management potential (0.53). The coefficients with performance were 0.36 (overall performance) and 0.33 (performance on the individual competency dimensions used at the centre).

I hope the point is made, and there is no need to quote study after study. The published evidence leads even the sceptics to state that 'given the predictive validities consistently reported in reviews, we would have to conclude that indeed assessment centers do work' (Klimoski and Brickner, 1987, p 244). This is the broad conclusion that is built upon in the salesperson's argument for assessment centres which can lapse into superlatives. In fact, the validity correlations that have been described imply a far from perfect prediction of performance, and it will be seen in Chapter 14 that they are further undermined when problems with the criteria (eg correlating assessment centre results with the resulting promotion decisions) and other detailed issues of how assessment centres work are considered. Nevertheless, for the advocate of assessment centres the qualifications are often ignored and the evidence seems to bear out their intuitive appeal.

Whilst there is a good deal of published evidence on assessment centres as predictors of performance, hard evidence of their developmental value is not so plentiful. There is a need for an empirical study to show that development has taken place, and that this development is tied to improved job performance. However, there is inferential evidence of the value of centres for development. For example, Schmitt *et al* (1986) demonstrate that attending the centre will help the person gain an accurate self-perception. People's self-perceptions after the assessment centre altered from their pre-centre perceptions for five of eight dimensions. The alteration was in line with their performance at the centre as seen by the assessors (whose reports had not been disclosed to the participants). Having an accurate self-perception must be a first step to development planning, even if it does not guarantee that the development will take place.

Finally, it is important to separate the validity of the centre as a measure of competencies from its validity as a predictor of performance. The centre's validity as a measure of competencies does not guarantee its validity as a predictor of success. After all, the competencies might not be those required for success. Conversely, a centre can be successful as a way of choosing people, but its success might not be a result of operating in the way intended by its designers (ie via the measure of particular competencies). It might still achieve predictive validity, but in some other way (eg by measuring a person's overall fit to the organization).

Justifying assessment centres: utility analysis

The studies that have been reviewed justify assessment centres on the grounds of their technical merits. In addition, Chapter 1 discussed their high level of acceptability. However, before making the considerable investment in the design and running of a centre, it might well be desirable to calculate the financial benefits. In order to do this, the methodology of utility analysis can be applied. It looks at the monetary gains from having a more valid personnel procedure. In the case of selection, the gains come from the organization recruiting people who are, on average, higher performers than would be recruited by a less valid procedure. This increase in average performance will yield either a gain in output if the same number of people are recruited, or a reduction in the payroll if fewer but higher performers do the same volume of work.

Utility analysis has been developed in the 1980s by Schmidt and by Hunter (eg Hunter and Schmidt, 1983; Schmidt *et al*, 1986) from earlier contributions by Brogden (1949), Cronbach and Glesser (1965), and Dunnette (1966). It is quite a complex procedure but, in the case of selection, the analysis is based on a knowledge of the accuracy of different methods of selection, and of how much people's performance can vary in a job depending upon their ability to perform it. For some jobs, it might be that everyone will perform equally satisfactorily and so the expense of any selection procedure is hard to justify. For other jobs, there will be a wide and readily apparent variation between the high and the low performer. The greater the potential variation in performance, the more point there is in investing in an accurate procedure for choosing between applicants. The analysis calculates the financial benefit of a more accurate procedure that raises the average level of performance of people.

The variation in performance can be expressed in monetary terms quite easily for some jobs. For example, the variation between salespeople is directly calculable in terms of the sales each of them makes. However, for many jobs, including managerial jobs, the direct measurement of performance in monetary terms is less easy. Schmidt *et al* (1979) provided a practical method for estimating the variations in these cases which resulted in a range of figures depending upon the job. This range, reported by Schmidt and Hunter (1983), was from 42 per cent to 60 per cent of the salary. To be conservative, they put their 'rule of thumb' estimate in monetary terms for the variation between high and low performers as 40 per cent of the salary for the job.

Apart from the variation in performance, it is also necessary to know the selection ratio (the number of applicants for each post). There is no point in having an elaborate selection procedure if all applicants must be hired. Finally, there has to be an estimate of the accuracy of different procedures. One way of obtaining this estimate is to hire groups of people using different procedures and to determine the differences in performance between the groups. Such studies are rare, but three are reported by Schmidt *et al* (1986). These studies showed that the use of cognitive tests in selection would raise the output of American public-sector employees by just under 10 per cent, or would allow the workforce to be reduced by just under 9 per cent.

Unfortunately, it is far from easy to conduct this kind of experiment, and most organizations must therefore estimate the accuracy of different procedures from a knowledge of their validities. The validities can be obtained directly by correlating people's performance on the selection procedure with their performance in the job. However, this means installing a new procedure and then waiting some time before people's performance can be measured. Clearly, this is not a great help if the objective is to decide whether to install the new procedure in the first place! In such cases, the validities of different procedures are estimated from meta-analyses. We have seen in the above section that the meta-analytic estimate of the assessment centre's validity might be put at 0.40. For comparison, the figure generally quoted for the interview is about 0.20 (0.19 is quoted by Reilly and Chao, 1982).

Knowing these figures, it is possible to work out the benefit from the assessment centre. For example, suppose an organization is choosing ten people from 50 applicants and is considering using an assessment centre instead of a simple interview, and suppose these people will each be paid £15,000 in their first year. The rule-of-thumb variation between high and low performance is 40 per cent of £15,000, ie £6,000.

The utility of the interview over random selection for each person hired is this figure multiplied by the validity of the interview (0.20) multiplied by the figure from statistical tables (for a full explanation of this calculation see Alexander and Barrick, 1987 or De Simone *et al*, 1986) that takes into account the selection ratio. For a selection ratio of 1:5 this figure is 1.40. The utility of the interview over choosing people at random is therefore £1,680 per person.

The same figures are used in the calculation of the utility of the assessment centre over random selection, except that the validity coefficient is now 0.40. This gives a utility of £3,360, and so the assessment centre yields a gain of £1,680 per person. With ten people, the gain is £16,800. This is a gain in the first year. Against this must be set the initial costs and greater on-going expense of the assessment centre as opposed to the interview. However, when the gain is finally added over the length of the person's employment, the net gains become very high. Assuming a length of service of eight years and an assessment centre cost of £2,000 per appointment, and assuming also that the interview costs nothing, the saving is: (8 [years] × £16,000) – (10 [people] × £2,000), ie £114,400. If service was only three years, the saving would be £30,400. As noted above, the saving will be either in terms of needing less staff to do the same job (an argument which applies more with managerial and administrative work) or in the greater productivity of the same number of staff (which will apply more, for example, with sales personnel).

The above estimate would be altered under more sophisticated approaches to utility analysis which take account of variables such as discount rates and taxes that affect other investment decisions (Boudreau, 1983; Cronshaw and Alexander, 1985). However, whatever the detailed amendments, it is clear that better procedures have an economic return. Indeed, the figures that come from utility analysis tend to stagger people by their size. To give a published example, Feltham (1988b) estimates that using the Civil Service assessment centre (CSSB) instead of an interview to select batches of 70 administrators saves the British government or taxpayer at least £1.8 million per batch.

In summary, assessment centres have empirical evidence on their side and this evidence can be turned into an estimate of financial returns. As we have seen, such an estimate generally shows that an assessment centre will save a great deal of money if it is substituted for less predictive methods of selection.

However, all this analytical evidence is far less important to a decision on whether to have a centre than the way it is extrapolated by those who advocate centres, or ignored by those who are not convinced. In other words, I think that the analytical arguments are far less influential in deciding whether to have an assessment centre than the more emotional arguments.

The emotional arguments in favour of assessment centres have been introduced in Chapter 1 in considering their seductiveness. Quite simply, they are an extremely plausible way of finding out about people's strengths and weaknesses on the dimensions of relevance to the target job, and once they are under way, assessment centres that are well designed will act as their own ambassadors. They sell themselves to line managers and participants. As Stevens (1985) found, the attitude of users is that the cost of the centre 'is minimal compared with the cost of not using them' (p 28). However, first of all the concept has to be sold. The arguments against them, together with counter-arguments, must now be considered.

Barriers to acceptance

Insufficient benefit

Assessment centres are complex to design. They are also time-consuming and resource-intensive to administer. There will clearly be many situations where no one other than a complete zealot would claim they are warranted. It might well be more appropriate to use a structured interview (Wright *et al*, 1989) and tests of aptitude and ability rather than an assessment centre. This will be the case, for example, in hiring lower-level trainees. However, there will be other situations when these are not convincing rivals to the assessment centres for external selection. They might be used as part of the centre, but do not bear close examination as an alternative to it. For external people, the obvious justification for assessment centres is that there is no other opportunity of viewing all the competencies that are important for the job.

The problem is that even when they would be thoroughly worthwhile, the organization's thinking about human resource issues must be sophisticated enough for the assessment centre approach to be seen as an appropriate rather than an exaggerated response. In particular, the assessment centre approach must be seen as worthwhile and valid by senior management. They are going to have to put in time in identifying the competencies, and to commit their staff to designing the exercises, being trained and acting as assessors. In addition, if the centre is for internal people, the managers must release the participants from their everyday work. Until there is a degree of sophistication, the advantages of assessment centres over other methods will not be appreciated. The highly visible direct costs of the centre will be more persuasive than the much less visible and unappreciated opportunity cost of not having it.

Alternatives for external selection

The cheapest alternative of all is not to have any assessment. It might be believed that the organization can get away with hiring people on probation and firing those who do not make the grade. In other words the probation period is the assessment. For example, this used very much to be the approach of the old-style City firms of stockbrokers, certainly up to the mid-1980s. I remember very well being told by one major firm of stockbrokers that they took people on, gave them a chance and fired them if it did not work out.

Even amongst its traditional advocates, such an approach seems likely to be on the wane. Apart from anything else, the reputations of organizations that hire and fire will lead to a decrease in the quality and quantity of applicants. In addition, with mergers, the macho approach might not fit easily with the parent company's philosophy. This conflict of style and values was evident, for example, between the traditional clearing banks and their new acquisitions. Finally, there is the cost of this approach. People who are found to be unsuitable are not free. It costs money to recruit them; they are paid during their stay; it probably costs money to get rid of them, and there is the opportunity cost of not having someone good in the post during their incumbency of it.

However, whilst this argument might be accepted, there will still be the argument that assessment could be done successfully by a cheaper method than an assessment centre. Quite rightly, people will ask whether there is a simpler way of finding out about people's competence than by using an assessment centre. Generally, line managers' reservations about assessment centres hinge around their faith in the existing methods of assessment. (What's wrong with the interview, or a thirty-item personality 'test', or graphology or whatever?) Many will be convinced that these methods are almost 100 per cent accurate and so the benefits from an assessment centre will be seen as too small to justify the cost. The problem is that the limitations to the alternatives are not appreciated by those who make the decisions.

One approach is to rely upon the right technical qualification or experience as a guarantee of competence, probably coupled with a quick interview. Of course, this might be adequate for some jobs, especially those which depend largely on technical expertise. One would not envisage an assessment centre for plumbers. However, for many jobs the non-technical requirements, such as interpersonal skills, still need to be assessed. For example, computer systems analysts need both technical and interpersonal competence if they are to work successfully, and an assessment centre exercise would reveal clearly how they interacted with their clients. In more managerial jobs, relying on experience suffers from two problems. Most obviously, the person might have failed to benefit from the experience and to develop his or her competence. Furthermore, whilst it is dangerous to overplay the uniqueness of organizations, competence in one organization's dimensions does not mean competence in another's. The dimensions might be different, or at least receive a different emphasis.

The greatest competitor to any innovation will be the interview. Despite the research evidence against it, many people have an implicit belief in the interview's utility, probably because they themselves carry out the interviewing: they believe they get it right most of the time. In fact, there is a body of evidence against the interview as the sole means of selection, and common sense tells us that, for many higher-level jobs, it cannot be expected to yield evidence on all the competency dimensions of importance. The interview might reveal some of the competencies, for example self-confidence. For that reason an interview will often be included in the assessment centre. However, the interview is quite obviously not best suited to assess other competency dimensions, for example organization and cooperativeness. Such competency dimensions as these are better observed via an assessment centre exercise. So interviews used on their own lack the logic and the empirical evidence that assessment centres provide.

Tests of aptitude and ability are another cheaper alternative to an assessment centre. They have a good track record as predictors of success (Schmidt and Hunter, 1981), and will often be appropriate for inclusion in the selection procedure. Of particular relevance are cognitive tests, such as those of reasoning ability. However, for higher-level jobs they should normally be an adjunct to the assessment centre rather than an alternative to it. Although the qualities the test measures might be very similar to one or two of the competencies needed for the job (especially analysis and solution finding), the assessment centre is still required to measure the remaining competencies. Furthermore, as Frederiksen (1986) points out, the simulation exercises measure a much broader conception of intelligence than the test. For a start, real-life problems do not come in a multiple-choice format. Even if the test measures a quality that is thought to lie behind many of the job's competency dimensions, the link between the source dimension and the performance dimensions might well not be proven or strong. Certainly, it will not extend to all competencies.

There is also the issue of acceptability to applicants. Just giving people tests carries the message that applicants are there to be processed as efficiently as possible. Nowadays many organizations are trying to give the message that they welcome applicants, and that the selection procedure will be more of a mutual exchange of information. In addition, in the unlikely event of tests and inventories being used on their own, (ie without any face-to-face component to the selection procedure, particularly an interview) there is the risk of making some gross error of selection. On the other hand, the assessment centre is quite a conservative procedure, and unlikely to let through anyone who will turn out to be a complete non-starter (Dobson and Williams, 1989).

The third potential alternative to an assessment centre is an inventory of personality. It might appear to give a sophisticated measure of the same competency dimensions that the assessment centre would address. However, behind the apparent sophistication, it is important to remember that all it can actually do is ask people to report on their own behaviour and preferences. The inventory should be carefully chosen to get at the relevant competency dimensions, but unfortunately they are installed all too frequently without a proper analysis of the competency dimensions required for successful performance. The invitingly labelled personality dimensions are all seen as important, whether or not they are actually related to success.

If the inventory's use is based on a proper job analysis, it might well be found that its coverage of the competency dimensions is incomplete. There is also still a great difference between a self-report of behaviour and a person's actual behaviour in a specific job. Assessment centres give a direct preview of behaviour, albeit in a somewhat contrived situation. Personality inventories have to rely on the faith that how people report their general past behaviour will be how they are going to behave in future in a particular job. The issue of generality is not entirely avoided by inventories that get people to report on their behaviour at work in general, rather than life in general. Even if they measure the person accurately, they still do so in situations in general. On the other hand, assessment centres get much closer to simulating the actual situation in which the person will be working. As such, they get much closer than a personality inventory to recognizing that behaviour is a function of both the person's general dispositions and the particular situation he or she is in.

Apart from their focus on the general, there is the obvious difficulty of people faking measures within the personality/interest realm, or just presenting a self-deluded view of themselves. This cannot be avoided by so-called lie scales, nor by ipsative measures. Perhaps these various problems explain why personality instruments do not have empirical evidence on their side. They are not good predictors of performance (Schmitt *et al*, 1984). In addition, they are not readily accepted by applicants as a proper alternative to simulation exercises. Certainly, I have anecdotal evidence that undergraduate applicants resent them, a view endorsed by Iles and Robertson (1989).

Alternatives to internal assessment centres

One use for an internal centre is to make promotion decisions. I would not argue that it is necessary or even desirable to have an assessment centre every time a promotion decision is to be made. Indeed, the main use of internal centres should be to encourage people's development. Nevertheless, there will be occasions when the apparent fairness of the assessment centre makes it desirable that it is used as the gateway to promotion. The main alternative is an assessment by the line manager, probably via the appraisal system. Line managers will often be idiosyncratic in their ratings, and might well focus on those competency dimensions that they value personally. For some managers these might be the interpersonal dimensions, whilst for others they will be the cognitive dimensions. If appraisal is used, some people might feel their prospects are blighted by a boss who does not like them. Others will complain of a boss who uses the appraisal process more accurately than the lenient bosses their colleagues enjoy. In contrast, the assessment centre has accuracy and logic which means that it will be seen as fairer when career decisions are being made. Everyone is assessed in the same exercises using a small team of highly trained assessors.

The disadvantage of using the centre for promotion is that it will become an object of fear and will demotivate those who fail. However, this might be outweighed by its demonstrable fairness. Certainly, exactly the same disadvantage applies to the other alternatives to the line manager's appraisal such as an interview, tests or personality inventories. These will not even be seen as fair, and really are not strong alternatives in terms of giving the right answers.

Austin (1986) observes that assessment centres will be an 'unnecessary and expensive luxury' (p 6) if senior executives have all the necessary information that is needed to make promotion decisions, understand that there are different criteria for success at different levels in the organization, and are able to monitor and assess employees against these changing criteria. Meeting these conditions is a tall order. They also emphasize that assessment centres are particularly useful when they focus on a job or job level that has different requirements from those of the participants' present job or job level. For example, the assessment centre is ideal for a bank looking for potential junior managers amongst its clerical staff, as clerks do not usually have a chance to demonstrate managerial attributes. The same logic applies to supervisors' assessment centres. Conversely assessment centres will seem less justified if the attributes are highly visible in the person's current job, and if there is confidence in the appraisal process.

The appraisal process might also be seen as an alternative to an assessment centre if the major purpose is people's development. The advantage of the assessment centre is that it can focus on the future. The exercises are in settings that the person will face in higher-level jobs, and the competency dimensions are those that apply to such jobs. In this way, it contrasts with appraisal which focuses on past behaviour. Even if the main concern is immediate development needs, these are likely to be identified much more accurately by the assessment centre approach, and in a way which will be owned by the person concerned. The assessment centre will have taken the person away from his or her job to focus intensively upon development needs as well as career aspirations, and the feedback can be carried out in a way that will result in the person owning the development plan.

Personality inventories might also be seen as an alternative method to encourage development. However, they would be much better seen as an adjunct to assessment centre exercises than as an alternative. Filling out the inventory will not have nearly the same impact upon people as taking part in simulation exercises. Even in the adjunct role, there is the danger that people hold the notion of a 'personality test' in awe. Feedback must be sensitive and tentative, and should certainly avoid the highly dogmatic approach of statements like 'The test says . . .'. This makes participants assume that having a particular disposition is not open to change, which is hardly a message to encourage development.

Expense

Assessment centres have highly visible direct and indirect costs. These might include consultancy fees for the centre's design, as well as costs for hotels, stationery etc for running the centre. More important will be the indirect costs in terms of managers' and participants' time. Indeed, Imada *et al* (1985) found in an international survey that 'by far the most consistent obstacle to implementing an assessment centre is the economic issue' (p 62). The organization might feel that it simply cannot afford these costs especially as the loss from not having the assessment centre is only that staff are less effective – they are not totally ineffective. With or without a centre, the work is still done, and the costs of not having one are hidden. On the other hand the development and running costs of having a centre are all too apparent.

In these circumstances, rather than demonstrating the 'telephone number' savings generated by utility analysis, it might be more productive to tailor the approach so that the actual costs of the centre are less threatening. For example, I had to design an assessment centre for an organization which had been using a panel interview. The centre was to cost no more in time than the interviewing procedure, which was based upon a board of three people that saw six candidates a day. I was able to design a one-day centre that still saw six people and used three assessors, but now they saw the candidates in a variety of settings across six hours, rather than in one setting for 40 minutes. Indeed, even the time available to interview each candidate was longer.

Too small an organization

An organization might be seen as being too small for an assessment centre. It might be that it has too few people at any level for it to be seen as worthwhile to have an assessment centre. To enjoy the benefits of a centre, such an organization might focus on the generic competency dimensions across a set of jobs rather than emphasizing the specifics of each job. The use of off-the-shelf exercises might also be investigated, but please see Chapter 6 for a discussion of this alternative.

Loss of power

The assessment centre might be seen as taking away the power of decision from some line managers or 'local barons', and putting it in the hands of the HR department. The centre will analyse people's strengths and development needs. Part of their development might well include movement to other jobs. This will prove unpopular with local managers when they lose their 'stars' to other parts of the organization. So to sell the assessment centre concept, it is clearly vital to carry along those with power by selling them the benefits, and ensuring that they will still feel in charge of the new system by helping to design and operate it. Certainly, the centre must not be seen as a way of the HR department taking more and more of the decision making from them.

Biding time

The old adage holds good that it is better to be told to introduce the HR enhancements by the Chief Executive rather than to be battling against a cynical Board of Directors. A top-driven approach is always more satisfactory, and it is certainly not going to be productive to try to introduce an assessment centre with top-level resistance. Centres take up a lot of time in their design, and – more importantly – they are resource-intensive to run. The initiative simply will not survive against the opposition of key stakeholders in the organization. Until the need is underlined to senior management by some problem, all of the arguments for assessment centres will be seen as academic. The status quo will feel comfortable, and will not be disrupted by intellectual argument. The champion of assessment centres will have to wait for a favourable opportunity to sell assessment centres as the solution to an obvious need. The opportunity might be provided by a set of people let in through the interview who turn out to be unsatisfactory, or it might be a difficulty filling posts with experienced people so that the organization has to turn to trainees with no real track record. It might simply be that competitors are using assessment centres, and so a decision is taken to try them out.

4: Project Management

Gaining commitment

Once it has been agreed to develop the centre, it is important to keep everyone committed. This means involvement and communication. It is important to involve people in the design of the centre and to make its purpose clear throughout the organization.

The major stages of design should be outlined and the major purpose should be made quite clear in a communication to the whole organization. Attention must be paid to the wording of any announcement, as an unfortunate impression at this stage will be hard to dislodge. For example, an internal centre that is meant to be developmental will be undermined if people attending it are called candidates rather than participants. The briefing documents for the centre are dealt with in greater detail in Chapter 8. For the moment, it is enough to note the importance of communication as part of the general process of involving people in the project.

The main means of involving line managers will be by getting them to take part in the job analysis and in the exercise design. People from across the organization should be included, and not just a group of HR trusties. It might be worthwhile to do some groundwork that is unnecessary from a technical point of view but that gets maximum involvement. For example, in determining the competency dimensions, representatives from all interested departments should be interviewed, and any job analysis questionnaire that is developed should be sent to as many people as possible. In two recent assignments, we sent the job analysis questionnaire to all managers in the organizations concerned, which meant 400 people in one case and 1,200 in another. The costs in terms of paper and of data entry were far outweighed by the benefit of being able to say that everyone was included in the analysis.

A representative sample of line managers should be involved in designing the exercises and in acting as assessors. Once they have been involved in the centre's design, they will be its ambassadors.

Any doubters should be won over by involving them in this way. It is very important that all interested parts of the organization are included. If this would mean more people than can be used for the exercise design, the remaining people should be brought in as assessors. This might mean having more assessors than are actually needed, but that is preferable to letting some parts of the organization disown the centre.

Giving a sense of ownership to line managers results in assessment centres passing the consultancy test of acceptability as a method of selection and of initiating development. It involves line managers and gives them the same belief that some of them have in the interview. The difference, of course, is that with assessment centres the belief is well founded. They pass the technical test of being a good way of finding out about people's strengths and weaknesses. The first step in this technical aspect of assessment centres is to specify the dimensions on which they must focus. This is the subject of the next chapter.

To summarize, it is vital that the centre is owned by the organization and is not seen as an HR enterprise. This means involvement and communication. It also means the centre's designer exercising the consultancy skills of listening and adapting the design to suit the needs of the line managers and participants. It is therefore better to avoid having too fixed an idea at the outset of how the centre is going to be.

Project stages

Designing and running an assessment centre is a complex project. It consists of a series of interlinked stages and sub-stages, as shown in Figure 4.

Once the project has been set up, the main stages are the job analysis, the design of the centre itself and of the development system, the training of assessors and role players, and an analysis of the centre's validity and the implications of its results in terms of general areas of strength and weakness for the organization. The remainder of this book, up to Chapter 14, goes through these stages of the assessment centre project.

Project personnel

The people involved in the assessment centre project will usually be as follows:

The co-ordinator. This person will usually be the 'champion' of the assessment centre initiative. He or she is most likely to be from the management development function of the organization.

Steering group. The co-ordinator probably needs to involve a small number of key people to oversee the project. They should be of board-level status, and will be in a position to endorse the project at its major stages (deciding the competencies; agreeing the assessment centre format, the budget and the assessors; agreeing policy on whether the primary purpose of the centre is selection or development, and on who should be invited to attend the centre and what happens afterwards; and agreeing the development programme).

Project team. They will carry out the detailed work with the co-ordinator. The team might well be just one other person who will help with the competency analysis etc, and will usually be from the management development function. Having such a team is strictly speaking optional as the co-ordinator might perform these tasks alone.

Assessment centre design teams. These will be teams of line managers who will work with the co-ordinator to design the exercises. They will have been picked to be representative of the whole organization.

Assessor group. A team of line managers, probably including the design teams, who will act as assessors. A fuller discussion is contained in Chapter 9.

Role players. They will be required for any one-to-one exercises and again there is a fuller discussion in Chapter 9.

It can be seen that getting to the stage of having an assessment centre involves a considerable number of people and a good deal of co-ordination.

Figure 4

Stages to the introduction of an assessment centre

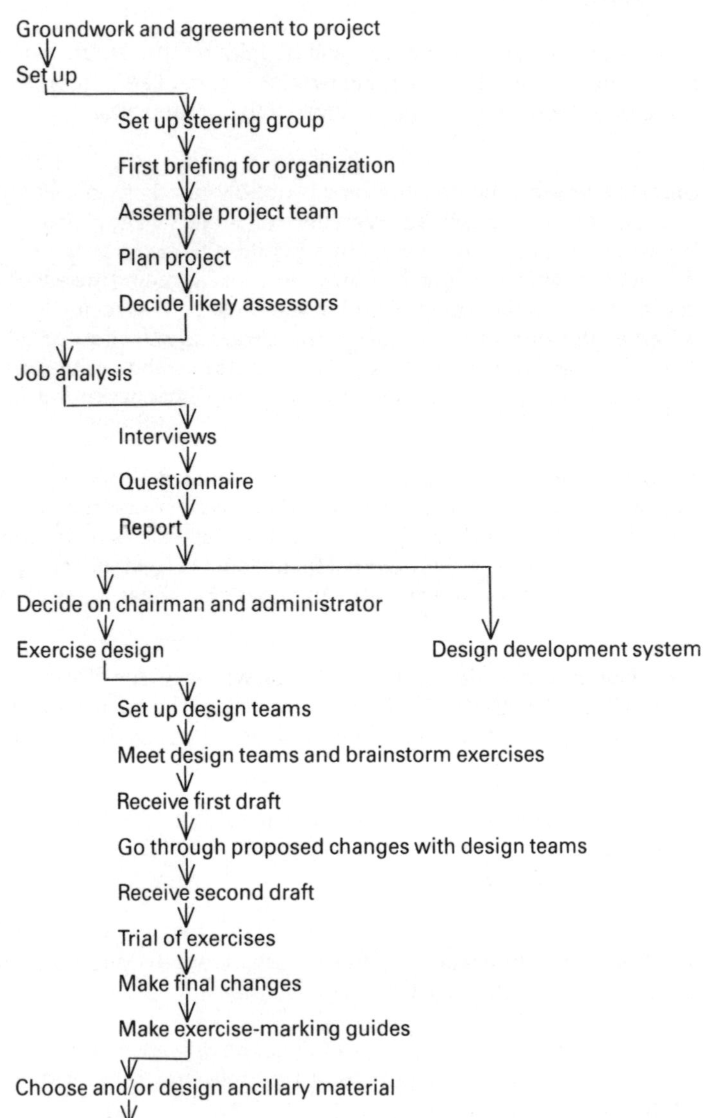

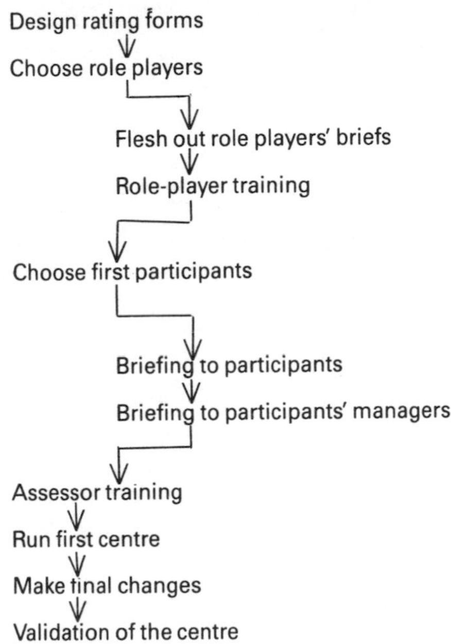

Project timetable

A rough timetable for the project is shown in Figure 5, page 44.

It can be seen that about six months will be required between deciding to have an assessment centre and running the first one.

Using consultants

It might be decided to call in a consultant to work on the design of the centre, especially if there is a complete lack of experience within the organization. The advantage of this is shown in a memorable quote by Finkle (1976), who says, 'As tempting as it may appear, the ready availability of group exercises is, in and of itself, hardly a case for a "do-it-yourself" approach to assessment centers any more than the availability of scalpel and suture recommends a "do-it-yourself" approach to brain surgery.' (p 882)

Perhaps consultants will only be engaged for particular stages in the design. For example, it will be worthwhile for someone who is really not sure about the process of analysing the competencies to

Figure 5
A Gantt chart of the project

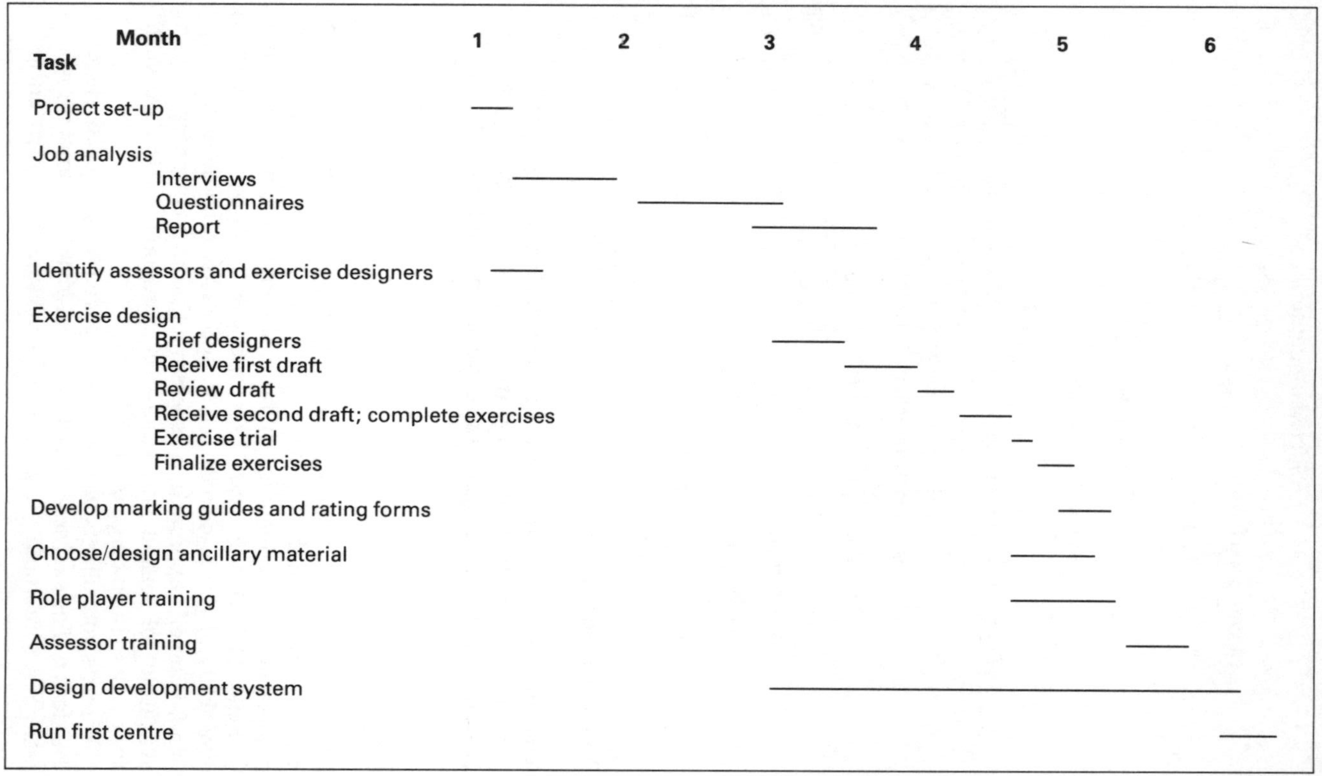

Task | **Month** 1 2 3 4 5 6

Project set-up

Job analysis
- Interviews
- Questionnaires
- Report

Identify assessors and exercise designers

Exercise design
- Brief designers
- Receive first draft
- Review draft
- Receive second draft; complete exercises
- Exercise trial
- Finalize exercises

Develop marking guides and rating forms

Choose/design ancillary material

Role player training

Assessor training

Design development system

Run first centre

seek consultancy advice. However, the same person might feel more confident in the process of exercise design.

I hope that this book will help buyers of consultancy to know whether they are speaking to someone who really does have expertise. Beyond that, it is good advice to ask for references from organizations with whom the consultant has worked, and to check that the people who will actually be operating the assignment have substantial experience. The well-known risk is being sold the project by the person with experience only to find that the operating consultant is the latest addition to the payroll. It would also be advisable to ask to see examples of the consultants' work. For example, if they are to do the analysis of the competencies, it is a good idea to be shown a competency list they regard as good before employing them. Certainly they should not try to create awe with the esoterically labelled methodology they employ.

5: The Competency Analysis

The starting point of the assessment centre project is to get a clear and accurate specification of what the centre is measuring. The word competencies has become the accepted label for what an assessment centre measures, and getting the list of competencies right is arguably the most crucial part of assessment centre design. If the list is wrong, people are being looked at against the wrong requirements, and there will be incessant problems in the design, development and operation of the centre. Indeed, the list is the hub of the whole assessment and development system. Time and resources put in at this stage will pay off. It should drive not just the assessment centre, but also appraisal, training and development (eg Treadwell, 1989). In addition, the recruitment and preselection system should be based on the competency dimensions revealed by job analysis. The list dictates the application form and the preliminary selection procedure. It can also exert an influence before preselection. For example, a recruitment advertising agency should be able to make use of the job analysis in framing an advertisement to appeal to people with the required qualities.

Defining a competency

There has recently been an upsurge in the attention paid to competencies. Undoubtedly this has made for greater potential sophistication in the way the requirements of jobs are specified. However, it is equally clear that there is a great variety in the quality of the lists that are produced. This is because of the lack of agreement on what competencies are and how to specify the competency lists. It often seems to be used as an umbrella term to cover pretty well anything that might directly or indirectly affect job performance.

The lack of agreement about what a competency is presents a problem for the job analyst because it can mean the analysis lacks a clear and coherent focus. The analyst is not sure exactly what is to be identified and so cannot discriminate between useful and not so useful information given by people being questioned about the job. It is also a problem when the assessment centre is developed because there is no clear model of the relationship between the different types of variable that might be measured at the centre. For example, one long list of competencies might include behaviours (eg behaving with sensitivity); their presumed causes (eg emotional stability); and their consequences (eg good staff management).

The umbrella definition of competencies stems from the pioneering book on *The Competent Manager* by Boyatzis (1982). Boyatzis distinguishes between functions, tasks and relevant competencies. For example there is the planning function, one of the tasks being determining the goals of the organization. The relevant cluster of competencies is the 'goal and action' cluster which is composed of efficiency orientation, proactivity, diagnostic use of concepts and concern with impact.

Boyatzis defines competency broadly as 'an underlying characteristic of a person'. It could be 'a motive, trait, skill, aspect of one's self-image or social role, or a body of knowledge which he or she uses'. Likewise Hornby and Thomas (1989) define competencies as 'the knowledge, skills, and qualities of effective managers/ leaders' (p 53). In contrast to competencies defined in these ways, Dulewicz (1989) notes that the dimensions assessed at assessment centres are clusters of behaviours. However, as he says, these 'have now been called "competencies" although they are not directly related to Boyatzis' model' (p 56). For example Dulewicz himself goes on to talk about using the assessment centre method in a national competency assessment scheme: the competencies are the dimensions and vice versa.

I think that it is far better to stick with the narrow definition of competencies as behavioural dimensions that affect job performance. They are behavioural repertoires that some people can carry out better than others. It is these behavioural dimensions that should be the focus of the job analysis. What matters to people's performance is the way they behave, and the job analyst must first of all find out the behaviours that distinguish high performance. It is only once these dimensions have been found that the analyst might try to speculate on the causes of behavioural differences.

Defining competencies as the behavioural dimensions that matter to job performance does not rule out traits, motives and dispositions because the distinction between these and the behavioural dimensions is false. It has been perpetuated by the recent invention of the term 'soft competencies' to refer to such qualities as creativity and sensitivity. They are contrasted with what are seen as more directly observable qualities like planning and organizing. This distinction was made, for example, by Jacobs (1989), who went on to claim that the soft qualities could not be measured by assessment centres but were of increasing importance to organizations in times of rapid change.

Soft competencies are traits, and the distinction between traits and behavioural dimensions is more apparent than real. The behaviour and the trait or soft competency are two sides of the same coin. For example, the trait of self-confidence can be said to lie behind whether the person behaves in a self-confident manner. However, it is only known that they have self-confidence because they behave self-confidently (Mischel, 1968, 1973). Exactly the same is true of creativity and sensitivity, which Jacobs quotes as soft competencies. The soft and any other competencies are only summaries of behaviour. People behave creatively (ie they produce original ideas to solve problems etc) and so we know they have creativity. People behave sensitively (ie they take account of others' needs etc), and so we know they have sensitivity. In the same way, a person is only known to have Boyatzis' efficiency orientation, because he or she behaves in the various ways used to indicate efficiency.

So defining a competency as a behavioural dimension encompasses traits, motives and dispositions, if it is recognized that these qualities are only convenient inferences from people's behaviour. Indeed, the titles of competencies might well be in the language of traits. An example of a list of competencies, which I believe is a reasonably good approximation to a list of generic management competencies, is contained in Figure 6 on the next page.

It can be seen that the competencies are clusters of behaviours. Their headings, such as self-confidence and incisiveness, aim to capture the essence of each cluster. Although the heading is in the language of a trait or ability that people possess, the competencies are dimensions of behaviour. The person behaves with self-confidence, and we only say someone has a trait (they have self-confidence) because of regularities in behaviour (they behave self-confidently). The competencies will be measured by the assessment centre exercises. People perform in simulations of the job and their performance is assessed in terms of the competencies that matter to the job.

Whilst the heart of the job analysis is the behavioural dimensions that distinguish performance, the job analyst might, of course, also be concerned to discuss the causes of behaviour. These might be

Figure 6

An example competency list

Breadth of awareness to be well informed
Develops and maintains networks and formal channels of communication, within the organization and with the outside world; keeps abreast of relevant local, national and international political and economic developments; monitors competitor activity; has a general awareness of what should be happening and what progress is being made.

Incisiveness to have a clear understanding
Gets a clear overview of an issue; grasps information accurately; relates pieces of information; identifies causal relationships; gets to the heart of a problem; identifies the most productive lines of enquiry; appreciates all the variables affecting an issue; identifies limitations to information; adapts thinking in the light of new information; tolerates and handles conflicting/ambiguous information and ideas.

Imagination to find ways forward
Generates options; evaluates options by examining the positive and negative results if they were put into effect; anticipates effects of options on others; foresees others' reactions; demonstrates initiative and common sense.

Organization to work productively
Identifies priorities; thinks back from deadline; identifies elements of tasks; schedules elements; anticipates resource needs; allocates resources to tasks; sets objectives for staff; manages own and others' time.

Drive to achieve results
Prepared to compromise to achieve a result; installs solution within timeframe; innovates or adapts existing procedures to ensure a result; takes on problems; suffers personal inconvenience to ensure problems are solved; comes forward with ideas; sets challenging targets; sets out to win new business; sets own objectives; recognizes areas for self-development; acquires new skills and capabilities; accepts new challenges.

Self-confidence to lead the way
Expresses and conveys a belief in own ability; prepared to take and support decisions; stands up to seniors; willing to take calculated risks; admits to areas of inexpertise.

Sensitivity to identify others' viewpoints
Listens to others' viewpoints; adapts to other people; takes account of others' needs; sees situation from others' viewpoints; empathizes; aware of others' expectations.

Co-operativeness to work with other people
Involves others in own area and ideas; keeps others informed; makes use of available support services; utilizes skills of team members; open to others' ideas and suggestions.

Patience to win in the long term
Sticks to a strategic plan; does not get side-tracked; sacrifices the present for the future; bides time when conditions are not favourable.

looked at in the assessment centre. However, they will not be examined via the assessment centre exercises. For example, the cause of a lack of self-confident behaviour might be a deep unresolved psychodynamic conflict. Alternatively, it might be a spouse who undermines the person's self-confidence. In fact, all manner of psychological variables as well as training and experience might lie behind the behaviour, but these cannot be observed directly at the centre. The cause of these behaviours can only be revealed by in-depth psychological interviews. Finding out the reason the person does or does not behave in a particular way matters because it will suggest the ease or difficulty of development.

In addition to the distinction between the behavioural competencies and the real causes of behaviour, there is also a distinction between the competencies and the roles performed in the job. The competencies deal with what behaviours people need to display in order to do the job effectively (eg sensitivity), and not with the job itself (eg staff management). The job itself consists of a set of deliverables, outputs or roles, each of which requires a number of individual competencies. Some lists of competencies confound these two by lumping together what people must be able to do with what they need to do it effectively. The result is a set of competency dimensions that are not independent, and a team of assessors who do not know what particular competency to credit with a particular piece of behaviour. For example, if someone exhibits the behaviour 'refrains from interfering unnecessarily with subordinates' work', assessors want to credit the competency of sensitivity, but they also want to give credit to staff management. This duplication helps give rise to a halo effect whereby marks are generalized across dimensions.

The aspects of the job should be a separate list. They need not be presented to assessors, but will be used by the exercise co-ordinator to ensure that the exercises are representative. The competencies and the aspects of the job can be tied together in the form of a grid such as that in Figure 7.

Apart from the behavioural competency dimensions, the job analysis might also reveal specific 'technical' skills and knowledge and abilities that are required for the job. Calling these competencies seems likely only to muddle the definition of a competency again, and it seems better to use a separate label. These knowledge skills and abilities apply particularly to jobs with a professional component, for example the job of a solicitor. Many of the behavioural competencies in Figure 6 will be necessary to perform satisfactorily as a solicitor. In addition, there are the specific technical skills and knowledge

Figure 7

Grid relating competencies to outputs

Output	Strategic Thinking	Problem Solving	Persuasion	Staff Management	Training and Development	Customer Service	Business Development
Competency							
Breadth of awareness	x	x		x			
Incisiveness	x	x	x	x	x		
Imagination	x	x	x	x	x	x	x
Organization		x		x	x	x	x
Drive		x	x	x	x	x	x
Self-confidence	x	x	x	x	x	x	x
Sensitivity		x	x	x	x	x	x
Co-operativeness		x	x	x	x	x	
Patience	x		x	x	x	x	

such as knowing the law of tort and how to draw up a will.

This professional knowledge is likely to be the result of, and perhaps can only be assessed by checking the possession of, particular levels of experience and qualification. However, it is important to note that what is really required is the professional skill and behavioural competency rather than experience *per se*. It will be important to build this information on professional requirements into a selection assessment centre by including an interview that focuses on people's experience, together, perhaps, with a review of a portfolio of their work if it is appropriate (eg in a creative job).

A model relating the variables that can be examined at the centre, and which might be uncovered by the job analysis, is presented in Figure 8.

Specifying the competencies

This book does not attempt to cover job analysis in detail. The various techniques are dealt with by Pearn and Kandola (1988), and by many textbooks on personnel management (eg Siegel and Lane, 1982). However, there are a number of specific points to be made in connection with the analysis for an assessment centre. These points revolve around the fact that the primary objective is to design, within an integrated management development system, processes for assessing people's levels of competence and developing their competence.

Focus on the future

One problem in deriving the lists is the danger of becoming bound to a particular methodology. It might be thought that job analysis has to be done in a particular way, for example via the repertory grid or the critical incidents technique. What is worse, these techniques might be seen as producing guaranteed results. They appear to be the royal road to competency analysis, but it can turn out to be a royal cul-de-sac. A major danger is producing lists based more on history than on the future. This can easily result from using a simple version of the repertory grid or critical incident techniques of interviewing. As Dulewicz (1989) observes, the grid must include 'a definition of the current manager who is likely to be successful in the environment envisaged for the future'. He continues: 'Involvement of top management in the final stages of discussion . . . is also imperative.' (p 59). This approach might be contrasted with one that proceeds by only examining the common denominators of people who have been

Figure 8

Relating the variables examined at the assessment centre

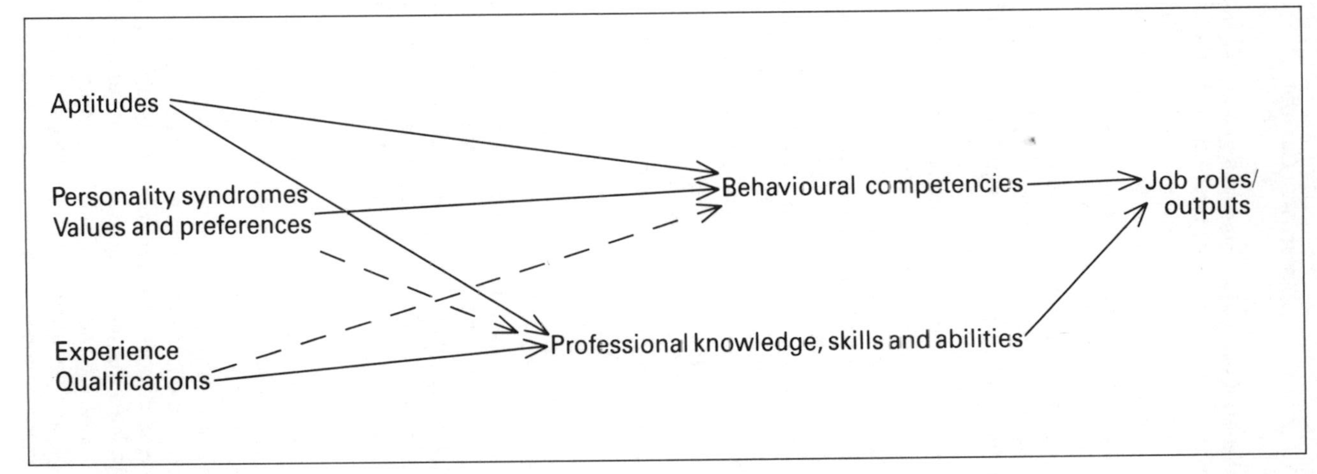

successful managers within business groups. Unless there is also a stage of checking out that 'have been' characteristics are also the 'will be' ones, the analysis might only be of historical interest.

This is a particular danger in the present conditions of rapid change that organizations face. Indeed as Kanter (1989) puts it, 'Managerial work is undergoing such enormous and rapid change that many managers are reinventing their profession as they go.' (p 85). The reason is that managers are increasingly having to deal with 'knowledge workers' who cannot be managed in traditional ways. They need to be shown that they are valued; they need to be listened to and their ideas implemented or the reasons for non-implementation discussed; they need to be given a sense of pride and opportunities to learn. Furthermore, what Kanter terms the 'postentrepreneurial' leaner, flatter organization emphasizes an array of networks that overlay any traditional hierarchy. Managers need breadth to know what is going on elsewhere in the organization, and they must take on a collaborative and strategic role. Generally, the recognition of the new environment in which managers operate (see for example Greatrex and Phillips, 1989, talking about BP, and Cockerill, 1989, about National Westminster) makes it essential that the competencies reflect present realities and the future rather than what might have been true historically.

Distinguishing types of competency

Boyatzis (1982) makes the distinction between competencies that differentiate between performance levels and threshold competencies, which are essential to adequate performance but do not give rise to high performance. The job analysis will certainly need to identify the competencies that differentiate the high performer from others in the job or job level. It will also need normally to discover threshold competencies. However, the list used for the assessment centre should not include dimensions or behaviours that are so mundane that everyone possesses them at the level of focus.

The job analysis will need to recognize the distinction between centres that are to measure readiness to perform a job tomorrow, and those that focus upon potential. If the focus is upon potential, the analysis should not include behaviours that everybody can be expected to learn between the time of the centre and the time when they are ready for the job. Such behaviours do not discriminate between people in terms of their potential. However, these behaviours might be included if the centre is to measure readiness to perform the job tomorrow, if only to point up immediate training needs.

Seeing the wood for the trees

It is important to focus on the level of generality that is appropriate to designing the assessment centre. It is easy to become obsessed with detail, but an analysis carried out to uncover the micro-skills of a job is very different from one carried out to design an assessment and management development procedure. It is pointless making distinctions between competency dimensions which are so fine that, although they are intellectually satisfying, assessors will never be able to follow them. To take a simple example, the competencies required for report writing and memo writing are often combined under 'written communication', and those for speaking to meetings and speaking one-to-one frequently come under 'oral communication'. However, the trick is not to become too general. For example, it might seem sensible to combine oral and written communication under the umbrella of 'communication skills'. The risk is that the list will be so general that a competency dimension could be assessed at a given level for very different reasons. The umbrella dimension of communication skills runs just such a risk. Some people are excellent at writing and not so good at oral communication (eg the caricature don). For others, the opposite applies. (It will be evident from Figure 6, page 49, that I have omitted both oral and written communication. The reason is that I believe they are both made up of the competencies in the table rather than being dimensions in their own right.)

A second example of an umbrella dimension is the one labelled 'personal factors' that appears in a number of organizations' lists. It is difficult to assess people under such a general title. A person can be strong on one personal factor (integrity was a sub-component in one list) yet weak on another (career ambition was another sub-component in the same list). The competency dimensions must therefore steer a middle course between making unnecessary distinctions and being too general to be useful.

Visible dimensions

The goal of the job analysis is to have a set of competency dimensions against which people can be assessed. Hypothetical psychological variables are inappropriate to such a list. For example, one organization had a list which included the dimension of self-monitoring. Assessors simply did not understand what it meant, let alone how they were to observe it.

Simplicity and brevity

The number of competency dimensions must be kept within bounds. Gaugler and Thornton (1989) demonstrate that the accuracy with which assessors classify and rate people declines as the number of dimensions is increased. Indeed Gaugler and Thornton argue for having just three to six dimensions, because this is the maximum number people can, in practice, make use of in reaching decisions. In their support, Russell (1985) demonstrates that assessors' ratings on 18 dimensions could be grouped into just four factors, the most important of which were interpersonal and problem-solving skills.

This research should be borne in mind if there is a temptation to produce a long list of dimensions. The number in practice probably needs to be greater than Gaugler and Thornton's recommendation, especially if the purpose of the centre is not just to make a decision, but also to give developmental feedback. However, I know one list that runs to 27 dimensions. This is far too long for assessment purposes. Assessors cannot possibly distinguish between and rate this number of dimensions, and the system is likely to fall into disrepute and disuse. Probably 12–15 competency dimensions is the most that can be used in the centre before it becomes unwieldy.

User-friendliness

It is important that the system of competencies and other types of variable is easy to understand. There should be a clear model of the relationship between the different types of variable that are being dealt with at the assessment centre so that people can see how they fit together. Furthermore, the system should be put across as far as possible in plain English. Even the word 'competencies' might be unnecessary for assessors. All that assessors really want is a list of what they are supposed to be assessing. The more complex the system becomes the more confused they will be. All that they need to focus on is the behavioural competency dimensions and the specific knowledge, skills, and 'technical' abilities for the job.

Defining dimensions

The competency dimension title (eg incisiveness) must be backed up with the behaviours that make up the dimension (eg gets a clear overview of an issue; grasps information accurately; relates pieces of information; identifies causal relationships; gets to the heart of a problem; identifies the most productive lines of enquiry; appreciates all the variables affecting an issue etc). Indeed the title is only the best summary that can be found for the cluster of behaviours. The competency dimensions are derived by finding the behaviours, clustering these together and giving the cluster an appropriate label. The order is not finding the dimensions and then defining them in terms of behaviours. Indeed the title for the dimension can be unhelpful, as it leads people to flesh out the dimension in their own ways. It is, of course, unrealistic, but it would be advantageous to omit the title and just give the dimension an index number followed by the indicators. The focus for the assessment centre and the management development activities is people's behaviour. It is the behaviours that assessors must learn and focus on, and which participants must develop.

Devise organization-specific competencies

Undoubtedly there are generic management competency dimensions. One such list is being compiled by Henley Management College, and is reported by Dulewicz (1989). These are middle-management competencies, which he calls supra-competencies. It is not in its final state but it consists of:

Intellectual:	Strategic perspective Analysis and judgement Planning and organizing
Interpersonal:	Managing staff Persuasiveness Assertiveness and decisiveness Interpersonal sensitivity Oral communication
Adaptability:	Adaptability and resilience
Results-orientation:	Energy and initiative Achievement-motivation Business sense

Dulewicz's senior manager competencies for BAT and Shell are very similar, in title if not in the required level, and I am sure most people could relate to the list. Equally, however, they could probably relate to the list published by Thornton and Byham (1982), which is:

Oral presentation
Oral communication
Written communication

Organizational sensitivity
Organizational awareness
Extraorganizational sensitivity
Extraorganizational awareness
Planning and organizing
Delegation
Management control
Development of subordinates
Sensitivity
Individual leadership
Group leadership
Tenacity
Negotiation
Analysis
Judgement
Creativity
Risk-taking
Decisiveness
Technical and professional knowledge
Energy
Range of interests
Initiative
Tolerance of stress
Adaptability
Independence
Motivation

This list is not applicable in its entirety to any particular job, although Thornton and Byham see virtually all as relevant to 'top management'.

Other lists that might be compared are those presented during 1989 in *Personnel Management* by major United Kingdom organizations. The summary lists are in Figure 9.

Without passing judgement on the merits of these various lists, there is clearly much overlap, which supports Dulewicz's belief in generic competencies. However, there are organization-specific competencies, and, most important, there is the problem of choosing between competencies in a generic list. The problem with generic lists is that they will be seen as applicable in their entirety. In this way, they are rather like personality descriptions, which people readily accept, whether they are actually based on the person's own inventory or another's.

Figure 9
Competency lists

Company	**Cadbury Schweppes**	**WH Smith**	**BP**	**Manchester Airport**	**National Westminster**
Author	**T. Glaze (1989)**	**R. Jacobs (1989)**	**J. Greatrex & P. Phillips (1989)**	**L. Jackson (1989)**	**A. Cockerill (1989)**
	Strategy	Written communication	Personal drive	Critical reasoning	Information search
	Drive	Oral communication	Organizational drive	Strategic visioning	Concept formation
	Relationships	Leadership	Impact	Business know-how	Conceptual flexibility
	Persuasion	Team membership	Communication	Achievement drive	Interpersonal search
	Leadership	Planning and organizing skills	Awareness of others	Proactivity	Managing interaction
	Followership	Decision making	Team management	Confidence	Developmental orientation
	Analysis	Motivation	Persuasiveness	Control	Impact
	Implementation	Personal strength	Analytical power	Flexibility	Achievement orientation
	Personal factors	Analytical reasoning skills	Strategic thinking	Concern for effectiveness	Self-confidence
			Commercial judgement	Direction	Presentation
			Adaptive orientation	Motivation	Proactive orientation
				Interpersonal skills	
				Concern for impact	
				Persuasion	
				Influence	

Source: *Personnel Management*, 1989 various issues.

To make the choices and ensure the inclusion of important competencies which are specific to the organization, I believe that it is important to go through a process of obtaining a list tailored to the particular organization. It is difficult just to make minor adaptations to a provided list and I recommend starting with a fresh sheet to derive a list that really does fit the particular level of job in the particular organization.

The process has a second major benefit in that the list is owned by the organization. As Greatrex and Phillips (1989) observed, the names of the 11 competencies produced for BP 'could be the universal requirements of any competent manager'. However, the 'crucial point' is that 'the behaviours listed within the clusters are cultural artefacts of the BP organization and expressed in terms of the language of the organization' (p 8).

Carrying out the analysis

There is no single way of deriving a list of competency dimensions or carrying out the rest of the job analysis. A theme of this book is the need to think flexibly around the particular situation, and to adopt the most appropriate approach. However, the job analysis will almost certainly include interviews. A typical way of getting at the dimensions is to carry out interviews with managers of the target job, job holders, and perhaps subordinates and 'customers' of the job. For example, to analyse the job of a bank branch manager, interviews would be held with those to whom the branch managers report. The focus would be what differentiates a good branch manager from a bad one both now and under future plans for the bank. Branch managers themselves would be interviewed to find out what they believe are the important behaviours that distinguish high from average performance. Subordinates could add further light on what makes a good manager, but interviewing them might well be controversial. Interviewing customers of the bank would also be most revealing, and should not prove so controversial, but it is rarely part of a job analysis.

In addition to what distinguishes high and low performers in terms of behaviours, the analysis must find out about the job itself. With job holders especially, interviews will find out what they do in their job and the typical situations they face. To help people describe their jobs, it can be useful to ask them to keep a diary for a week and fill in what they have been doing each half-day. At the end of the week, they would add any other aspects of the job not covered. The diary can be used to help identify the major types of situation in the job, as well as the major outputs and roles. For example, the list might include one-to-one meetings with customers, fellow managers and staff, as well as group negotiations and dealing alone with paperwork. This information can be used to start deciding the exercises that should be designed to simulate their work.

It is best to start with one-to-one interviews in a job analysis. However, after about 10–15 interviews with any particular type of respondent (eg managers of the job, job holders etc) the information becomes repetitive. At this point it can be more productive to collate the notes from the single interviews and then to interview pairs or groups of people to check the information. The pairs might be used to draw out any differences that are suspected between different categories of job. For example, there might be suspected differences between departments, or between head office and satellite offices.

In interviews, especially with the managers of the job, it is crucial to focus on anticipated changes in the job and its requirements. For example, branch banking has clearly changed to a much more proactive, sales-oriented, customer-oriented, risk-acceptant profile, from a profile that was pretty well the opposite. If the job analyst a few years ago had concentrated on the job as it was and not as it was about to be, the assessment centre would quickly have been assessing against a historical template!

The need to incorporate the future means that people at the highest levels of strategic thinking in the organization must be interviewed. Incorporating the views of these people not only adds crucial information to the analysis, but it also involves them psychologically in the project.

In carrying out any of the interviews, I do not believe it is essential to use a particular methodology, for example, the repertory grid technique or the critical incidents technique. These are means to an end, and they might not be productive, especially when senior people are interviewed. The goal is to find out where these people see the organization going and what the requirements of managers will be, given that scenario. How the goal is achieved does not really matter.

Having carried out all the interviews, the next task is to derive a preliminary list of competency dimensions. Whatever specific technique of interviewing was used, the majority of interviews will have elicited the positive and negative behaviours that differentiate levels of performance. These behaviours must now be grouped into the competency dimensions. There are various ways of going about this. The first is to cut out obvious duplicated statements of behaviour, and then present the rest in the form of a job analysis questionnaire. The responses are factor analysed to yield the competency dimensions.

This type of questionnaire is inevitably going to be rather long. Little is lost from grouping small numbers of the items into obvious subdimensions, and factor analysing these. Either way, the factor analysis will be of people's self-ratings on the competency dimensions or items. It should not be of their ratings of the importance of the items etc. The reason is that quite disparate items might be equally important and would thus come out on a single factor.

After this statistical analysis, the groupings of indicators that appear under each empirical factor should be inspected to make sure that they appear to be psychologically homogeneous and yet distinct from the other groupings or competency dimensions. The factors should be rational and intuitively sensible. It is important to be very well versed in the procedure being used, which should be seen as an assistant not a master. The list from statistical analysis should be adjusted so that it works in practice. The results do not have to be followed slavishly however counter-intuitive they may be. In all, it is vital to remember the purpose of the analysis. It is to derive a list of competency dimensions that will drive the assessment and development process. Assessors must be able to understand it, and management development staff must be able to design their systems around it.

A particular problem with lists derived by statistical analysis is competency dimensions that jumble up quite disparate indicators. An example is one organization's dimension entitled 'direction' which is made up of the following behaviours: being able to tell others what they must do and confront performance problems; being able to plan, organize, schedule, delegate and follow up. These are quite clearly very different indicators that do not group logically under one dimension. There are aspects of self-confidence, and of organizing ability. The risk with jumbled competency dimensions is that assessors will become confused. For example if they see a participant confront a performance problem, they will want to give credit to the dimension of self-confidence as well as to the participant's direction. It is vital that the final list is coherent enough to bear close examination by a cynic.

Apart from ensuring an homogeneity within competency dimensions, it is important to make sure that the distinctions between dimensions that the statistical analysis has made can also be made by assessors. For example, a job analysis I carried out distinguished between self-confidence and assertiveness. I am sure that these are separate dimensions and that someone could be highly self-confident but not very assertive and vice versa. However, assessors found the distinction hard to assimilate, and, in retrospect, it might have been better not to make it.

The final draft list of competency dimensions from the interviews and questionnaire will need to be ratified by the senior policy-makers within the organization, who should, once again, make sure that the future requirements of the organization are covered. Once the final list of competency dimensions has been made, it can be helpful to group them under broader headings. For example, a recent job analysis I carried out clustered the dimensions under the headings of information management, self-management, and people management. Similarly, BP cluster their dimensions under achievement orientation, people orientation, judgement, and situational flexibility.

Job roles

The questionnaire will also be used to obtain further information on the job itself. It will be used to finalize the list of roles or major outputs that the job involves. Frequently, the analysis will be covering a grouping of jobs which it makes sense to deal with generically, but which only have some roles in common and some that are different. This will be particularly true when the target is a job level, such as middle management, rather than a narrowly defined job. For example, some specific jobs at a given level will include business development as a role, whereas others will not.

The analysis can uncover the actual similarities and differences between jobs and job levels. It will show exactly how valid it is to treat the jobs separately. This will be highly useful information in carrying out the succession planning and career development process that will be a major follow-up to the centre.

Methodologies

It is easy to be beguiled by a particular methodology, and to lose sight of what it is doing fundamentally. The importance of focusing on the future has already been discussed. A method should not just be a large pooling of ideas about the requirements of the past. It should gain a few key people's ideas about the future. Similarly, it is important to beware of techniques that rely too much on managers' views of psychology. For example some approaches to job analysis get managers to relate competencies to job roles. This can result merely in a statement of the obvious. It is the job of the expert to challenge and question conventional wisdom. For example, if one of the competencies is incisiveness and one of the roles is problem solving, most people will see incisiveness as essential for problem solving. There is no need to spend a lot of time and energy getting a sample of managers to confirm this fact. Furthermore, this pooling of conventional views might miss the fact that incisiveness is just as necessary as interpersonal competencies if managers are to succeed in their role and developing their staff. This might not be obvious from a pooling of conventional wisdom.

No amount of apparently sophisticated statistical analysis can change the status of the data that goes into the analysis. The old adage of 'garbage in garbage out' applies. It is important to step back and examine the fundamentals of the technique to ensure that it cannot be accused of 'garbage in'.

Constant review

It is vital that the list of competencies is not static. It should be kept under review as the definition of a high performer varies. For example, David Duffield, Group Personnel Manager of National Westminster, said in an interview with Crabb (1989), 'We have done a lot of work . . . on the skills and competencies which are very important in the bank . . . And we're constantly looking ahead to see how these things are likely to change.' (p 37). Similarly, Greatrex and Phillips (1989) talk of BP recognizing the importance of checking their model and its validity 'about every two years to ensure it still reflects the company's needs' (p 39).

6: The Exercises

The grid of exercises

The heart of an assessment centre is the simulation exercises. The job analysis will have revealed the typical situations faced by people in the job (eg customer meetings). It will also have made clear what the main roles or outputs are (eg customer relations; business development) in these situations. The exercises are set within the organization and aim to simulate these situations and require the same outputs. For example, there might be a one-to-one exercise with a customer which gets the participant to maintain the relationship with the customer and to try to expand the business with the customer. To perform effectively, the participant will have to use a selection of the competencies revealed by the job analysis. In this way, the exercise design and job analysis cross-validate each other. If the job analysis competencies are correct and the exercises are well-designed as simulations of the job, then it will be possible to see the competencies in people's performance of the exercises. If the competencies cannot be observed in the exercises then either the exercise design or the job analysis is wrong.

The choice of exercises should depend solely on the findings of the job analysis, subject to practical constraints. An exercise should not be included just because it is usually found in assessment centres. For example, leaderless group discussions and in-trays are usual in assessment centres, but if they do not simulate the target job or job level they should not be part of the assessment centre. They will give access to irrelevant competency dimensions and deny access to the relevant. Conversely, a novel type of exercise certainly should be included if it is practical and would be a good simulation of the job. For example, in an assessment centre I helped design to choose supervisors for an engineering company, each participant was given six apprentices who had to be instructed on a method of working to make a simple piece of equipment. The participants then had to supervise the apprentices actually making the equipment. It worked very well as an exercise, and was certainly much better than a leaderless group discussion, which would not have been relevant.

The mix of exercises must take into account the eventual timetable and the available resources in terms of assessors and role players. For example, there will be great difficulties if the centre consists of a series of one-to-one role plays. Unless there is one role player and assessor per candidate, participants who are not taking part in a role play must be occupied with some other activity. This might well be possible if the centre is developmental. The time could be used, for example, to get people to consider their own performance in the last exercise, perhaps including a group discussion of the issues raised. The time might also be used for individual consideration of career aspirations etc. However, if the centre is to be used for selection, the time will be less easy to use, and it is usual to have one or more written exercises that can be run in parallel to the one-to-one exercises.

The full set of exercises should fit together in a workable timetable, simulate key aspects of the job and give an adequate measure of the competency dimensions that are critical to the job. There is some debate about the abilities of assessors to assess by dimensions as opposed to by exercises (see Chapter 14). However, at this design stage, care should be taken to ensure that the dimensions are properly represented across the suite of exercises. Then, even if assessors only give an overall score for each exercise, that score should represent the different dimensions.

To ensure that the competency dimensions are properly covered, it is usual to have a grid of dimensions against exercises, and to check off which dimensions will be shown by each exercise. Fine tuning of exercises is possible to bring out under-represented dimensions. An example of a grid of competency dimensions by exercises is presented in Figure 10.

All competency dimensions should be measured at least twice, and preferably three times. If some dimensions are clearly more important to the job, and therefore to anyone's suitability for the job, then they must be measured three times, and a fourth time would be an advantage.

Types of exercise

Written exercises

These exercises are simulations of the type of written work that might

Figure 10

Example of a grid of competencies by assessment techniques

Competency	Group Neg'n	Group Problem	In Tray	Analysis	Sub 1 to 1	Interview
Breadth of awareness to be well-informed Develops and maintains networks and formal channels of communication, within the organization and with the outside world; keeps abreast of relevant local, national and international political and economic developments; monitors competitor activity; has a general awareness of what should be happening and what progress is being made.		X	X	X		X
Incisiveness to have a clear understanding Gets a clear overview of an issue; grasps information accurately; relates pieces of information; identifies causal relationships; gets to the heart of a problem; identifies the most productive lines of enquiry; appreciates all the variables affecting an issue; identifies limitations to information; adapts thinking in the light of new information; tolerates and handles conflicting/ambiguous information and ideas.	X	X	X	X		
Imagination to find ways forward Generates options; evaluates options by examining the positive and negative results if they were put into effect; anticipates effects of options on others; foresees others' reactions; demonstrates initiative and common sense.	X		X	X	X	
Organization to work productively Identifies priorities; thinks back from deadline; identifies elements of tasks; schedules elements; anticipates resource needs; allocates resources to tasks; sets objectives for staff; manages own and others' time.		X	X	X	X	
Drive to achieve results Prepared to compromise to achieve a result; installs solution within timeframe; innovates or adapts existing procedures to ensure a result; takes on problems; suffers personal inconvenience to ensure problems are solved; comes forward with ideas; sets challenging targets; sets out to win new business; sets own objectives; recognizes areas for self-development; acquires new skills and capabilities; accepts new challenges.		X	X		X	X
Self-confidence to lead the way Expresses and conveys a belief in own ability; prepared to take and support decisions; stands up to seniors; willing to take calculated risks; admits to areas of inexpertise.	X	X	X		X	
Sensitivity to identify others' viewpoints Listens to others' viewpoints; adapts to other people; takes account of others' needs; sees situation from others' viewpoints; empathizes; aware of others' expectations.	X		X	X	X	
Co-operativeness to work with other people Involves others in own area and ideas; keeps others informed; makes use of available support services; utilizes skills of team members; open to others' ideas and suggestions.		X	X		X	X
Patience to win in the long term Sticks to a strategic plan; does not get side-tracked; sacrifices the present for the future; bides time when conditions are not favourable.	X		X	X		X

be undertaken by the target-level job holder. They are not abstract tests of psychological abilities. Apart from their validity, they have the practical advantage that they are completed by the participants on their own, and so they are a great help to timetabling. Their disadvantage is that too many such exercises become dull for the participants.

Within the category of written exercises, there are the following specific types of exercise:

In-trays. The most familiar written exercise is the in-tray, which simulates the typical pile of papers that might confront a job holder, for example, on return from a business trip or holiday. Items should be targeted on particular competencies, and it should be made clear to participants that the in-tray is not simply a test of delegation. If the person over-delegates, then it will be difficult to gain any useful information from the exercise on most of the competencies it was meant to measure. If, for example, the item that should have revealed the person's incisiveness is delegated, then no conclusion is possible about incisiveness.

The ability to set priorities can be measured via the in-tray by collecting the participants' out-tray every 15 or 30 minutes, and time-stamping each collection. This is much better than asking people to write out priorities on a sheet. The sheet alerts them to the need to set priorities, and it remains unknown whether they would actually carry out work in the priority order they have indicated.

In-trays can test interpersonal competencies, as well as cognitive competencies such as imagination. For example, the in-tray might require the participant to write a memo showing self-confidence and a letter requiring sensitivity.

Analytical exercises. The second well-used type of written exercise involves the participant doing a piece of analytical work. Such exercises are especially susceptible to the problem of favouring people from a particular department or with a particular background. For example, in a bank's assessment centre it would be unfair to include an analytical exercise that would be easier for people with a background in reviewing loan applications. The exercise must involve an issue which is even-handed to all participants.

Written components to interactive exercises. There might also be a written component to the interactive exercises. For example, participants might be asked to write a memo to their boss on the outcomes of the group discussion, or write a file note on the results of the subordinate one-to-one. This can be valuable in that it provides concrete evidence of the person's cognitive competencies in the interactive exercises, and removes any ambiguity about whether someone might have been extremely good at, for example, breadth of awareness, but said very little because of a lack of self-confidence.

One-to-one exercises

These exercises involve role players who will play, for example, the customer, subordinate or boss while the participant plays the part of the target-level job holder. For example, in one institution with which I worked, being able to deal with highly confident seniors was an important part of the job under consideration. We therefore had a role play exercise in which the participant had to negotiate with a bombastic senior. In other organizations, the meetings might be with outside contractors, government agencies etc. The exercise might be essentially one of fact finding and decision making, or it might involve negotiation. The choice of setting and roles or outputs will depend on the job analysis.

There might be a temptation to get another participant to do the role player's job, but this will be inadvisable if there is any element of competition to the centre. However, it is a possibility if the centre is truly developmental, and if everyone is allowed to take the role of the job holder so that they feel they have had the chance to derive equal benefit from the centre.

The disadvantage of one-to-one exercises is the need for role players. They add to the resources needed for the centre, and the exercises are time-consuming to run. However, they add realism to the centre, and this might well make their costs worthwhile.

Group exercises

The group exercises should replicate the key types of group with which people in the job will be involved. The major options are a problem-solving and a negotiating group. Negotiating group exercises give each participant a role. For example each might represent a different department negotiating with each other for office space. On the other hand, problem-solving group exercises might involve all the participants working from a common brief, with no one assigned as the leader, or leadership might be rotated.

Good early examples of the two main types of group exercise are provided by IBM, and described by Cascio (1982). IBM's negotiation exercise got each participant to champion a candidate for promotion. They were required to make a brief presentation of their candidate and then lead the group discussion. Nowadays there are many imitations of this exercise. IBM's problem-solving exercise asked the participants to work together as a group to operate a manufacturing company, without giving them any assigned roles.

It is particularly important only to have a negotiating group if it is relevant to the job. If it is decided to have this type of exercise, it is very important that the briefs given to the participants are approximately even in terms of the weight of the arguments they contain. This is easier said than done.

It might be that a problem-solving group is more relevant. One option is to have such a group in the leaderless format. However, this carries the particular difficulty that the strength of the person who turns out as leader will depend on the strength of other group members. A reasonably strong person will appear weak if all the others are very strong indeed. I think that it is far better to revolve the leadership, so that each person can be assessed in the role. For example, each participant might have their own problem, which they introduce to the group, lead the group discussion, and then sum up. I also advocate having a chairperson with a very light touch (probably the centre's administrator or chairperson), who ensures that nobody completely dominates the discussion, and who draws in any obvious non-participants. This resolves the question of whether a non-contributor is saying nothing because he or she lacks cognitive skills and has nothing to say or because of a lack of self-confidence.

Innovations in exercise design

Three new developments in assessment centre design are described by Bedford (1987), and might be found useful in exercise design. First, he draws attention to a study by Therrien and Fischer (1978), which assessed empathy using a paper-and-pencil method rather than a one-to-one role play. They constructed a series of statements which were either spoken by role players in a one-to-one exercise or presented to participants in a written form requiring a written response. The two types of presentation elicited very similar responses from participants. The finding could be used to justify including in an in-tray items that measure interpersonal skills. However, I do not think it should be the basis for a major departure from the overall approach of having direct simulation exercises. It is important to have participants perform in oral as well as written simulations of the job. Otherwise, the assessment centre could end up as a series of written tests. Apart from anything else, these might well fail the consultancy objective of acceptability to participants.

Another development is the use of video vignettes which present participants with the videotaped lead-up to a situation (for example an argument between employees) to which the participant (acting as the supervisor) must make a verbal response. This seems a good way of preserving fidelity, whilst ensuring that participants are presented with a consistent 'situation'. However, in isolation, it loses the richness of the full interactive exercises, and should be used as the lead-in to a full one-to-one exercise rather than a substitute for it.

The third novel type of exercise considered by Bedford breaks a complex situation down into a series of small parts to which participants respond. For example, The Ontario Provincial Police Academy simulate a high-speed car chase, and require participants to make a series of quick decisions, each of which is recorded and marked. In the managerial setting, it would be possible to have a business exercise that presented participants with sets of choices, each set focusing on a particular competency.

Exercise production

Exercises can be produced internally by the HR department. This avoids depending on others' co-operation, but it has the major disadvantage that no one is carried along with the centre's design. The alternative is to set up design teams of line managers to design the exercises, along with an HR co-ordinator. Unless there is a particular reason for not using it, I would strongly advocate this alternative. The line managers can help with the hard detail of exercise design and will serve as assessors. They should be carried along from the start of the exercise design.

The production will start with the HR co-ordinator deciding which line managers to involve as designers. I have found it helpful then to get exercise designers together as a group at the start of the exercise design phase. This allows any worries they might have to be discussed and tackled early. There should then be a second group meeting of exercise designers, at which ideas for the exercises are generated. I would advise having teams of two exercise designers for each exercise. By the end of the meeting, it should be possible to visualize the different exercises in sufficient detail to generate the preliminary grid of exercises against competency dimensions.

Drafting meetings
Each design team must meet with the co-ordinator to sort out the detail of their individual exercise. About two hours will be required for these meetings, after which the designers should go away to put some flesh on the bones of the exercise. This will mean differing amounts of work depending on the exercise. The written exercises are probably the hardest, together with a group negotiation exercise. The co-ordinator might need to give designers of these exercises some extra help. One-to-one exercises are generally more straightforward to design, as are group problem-solving exercises.

Exercise writing
In writing the exercises the goals are to have proper simulations of the target job, to use the correct format, to elicit the competency dimensions, to be fair, and to ensure that different levels of competency on the dimensions can be graded.

Proper simulations. The exercises should be clear simulations of the target-level job within the organization. This will ensure that their content relates to the job, and it will help ensure that they are predictive. It will also help to gain their acceptance by assessors and participants. For example, a subordinate one-to-one exercise might get the participant to discuss with the role player an inadequate piece of work by the role player; a customer one-to-one exercise might simulate the initial meeting with a prospective customer.

This approach contrasts sharply with having exercises that appear to show the competency dimensions but which do not try to simulate the target-level job. For example Rothwell (1985b) describes the inclusion of management games in the exercises, and gives as examples 'the well-known "Mast" exercise using Lego blocks, or the "Shipwreck" or "Desert Survival" game' (p 94). She goes on to comment that open-air exercises are 'more appropriate for graduate trainees or first line managers. Nevertheless, indoor versions of them for senior managers, using cardboard boxes and paper clips can provide useful diagnostic and self development exercises' (p 94).

An example of this type of exercise in use for graduate selection to a commercial organization was described by Hagedorn (1989). The organization was described as having a two-day assessment centre, the second day of which 'was like one of those army survival courses where teams had to work out how to get a bomb and all their equipment across a six-foot high electric fence in 45 minutes or cross a ditch full of piranhas'.

I do not favour this type of exercise for a number of reasons. One pessimistic reason for having good simulations is that assessors are not particularly good at assessing the competency dimensions they are supposed to be assessing, as Chapter 14 will show. They tend to lapse into assessing overall performance. If they are assessing performance in a direct simulation of the job, the assessment is still likely to predict job performance (Herriott, 1988). On the other hand performances with Lego or piranha-filled ditches might bear no relation to job performance. A second problem is that these exercises do not give a preview of the job to applicants, nor do they emphasize the relevance of the centre to internal participants. Thirdly, it is far easier to ridicule the relevance of performance at the centre if it is in a non-simulation exercise. Anyone who does not like their assessment by these exercises can reject the whole basis of the assessment.

Format. The exercises should not be written as if they were examinations. Instead, they should place the participant in a situation, such as the manager sitting down to tackle his or her in-tray, preparing to meet a customer or subordinate etc.

The written exercises will consist of the set of papers for the participant, together with instructions to the administrator, for example on the times to give out additional papers and collect out-trays. One-to-one exercises consist of the set of papers for the participant, together with the additional brief for role players. Group exercises are made up of the set of papers for participants, together with notes to guide the chairperson if one is involved in the exercise. The participants' papers for the group exercise will frequently consist of some that are common to all of them, and some that are unique to each of them. An example of one person's brief in a fairly simple group problem-solving exercise is contained in Figure 11.

Eliciting dimensions. There should be sufficient evidence on all of the participants for assessors to judge their strength in each of the competency dimensions targeted by the exercise. It is best to think through different ways that people might undertake the exercise, and decide whether it gives good evidence of the target dimensions. The grid of competencies by exercises might require revision as the exercise design progresses.

The goal of eliciting adequate evidence is more elusive than it might appear at first sight. A common pitfall is that the exercise may not oblige participants to reveal their strength in the competency dimension. It might be optional in the exercise whether the person

Figure 11

Example of a group problem-solving brief

The example is a hypothetical exercise for a retailer. The competitor who is mentioned on the next page would be the name of an actual competitor.

Area Manager's Meeting Exercise

Instructions

1. Time Limit: 1 hour 30 minutes

2. You are the six area managers from the North-West Region. The areas are:

- Merseyside
- Manchester
- Cumbria
- Peak District
- North Wales
- Pennine.

You will be the participants at the quarterly area managers' meeting to be held in FIFTEEN minutes' time. Each of you has a problem to be discussed at the meeting. When it is the turn for your problem to be discussed you should present it briefly, lead a discussion of it, and sum up at the end of the discussion. The meeting will then move on to the next manager's problem.

3. The exercise is in three parts.

   The first part lasts FIFTEEN minutes and is for you to read and familiarize yourself with your brief.

   The second part lasts ONE hour and involves each of you presenting your problem to the others in the group, and leading a discussion of it for TEN minutes. The discussion will be chaired by the Regional Manager, who is well known for taking a back seat at this kind of meeting. Normally, she just asks people to take their turn in leading the group, and will enforce the ten-minute time-limit strictly.

   The third part lasts FIFTEEN minutes. You will be asked to write a report on the discussion of your problem which can be faxed to your Assistant Manager, before you leave on a one-week business visit to an exhibition in Vienna.

Area Managers' Meeting Exercise

Manchester area instructions

You are the Manchester Area Manager.

You have FIFTEEN minutes to read, analyse and make notes on your problem as stated below, so that you are ready to brief the other managers on it and lead a discussion of it. Your problem will take up TEN minutes of the meeting.

The problem that you face in the Manchester area is the very severe competition from *a competitor* who has opened up just down the road from you (see attached map). With a combination of *the competitor's* special offers and marketing drive, the competition is having a noticeable impact on your monthly figures, as shown on the attached sheets. An analysis of the competitor's products and prices compared with ours is also attached.

You need to get ideas from your fellow-managers for a local marketing campaign, or for some other response to the competition that is in line with company policy.

Area Managers' Meeting Exercise

Part Three instructions

You have to leave in FIFTEEN minutes for a one-week visit to an exhibition in Vienna. Before you leave, you should write a fax for your Assistant Manager that summarizes the results of the discussion of your problem for him or her.

demonstrates it or not. The problem comes to the fore in group exercises. It is very important that the participants have every chance to demonstrate their strengths on the target competency dimensions. For example, suppose there is a simple group problem-solving exercise for which all participants have a common brief, and which they are left to get on with, observed only by the assessors. If the exercise was meant to measure breadth of awareness and someone says nothing, it is unclear whether it shows a lack of breadth or a lack of self-confidence.

In many cases, this issue can be overcome by distorting the exercise. For example, as we have seen, participants could have their own problems that are brought to the group for discussion. The instructions might call upon them to summarize their problem and then to lead the group discussion, summarizing the results at the end of the exercise, perhaps in a memo to their boss. It is then possible to be much more certain about the exercise as a measure of, say, breadth and self-confidence than if everyone simply took part in a group discussion.

The same problem occurs in an in-tray with instructions which enable some items to be missed. The missing items do not necessarily mean the person is weak in the competency dimensions they were meant to measure. Instructions need to be worded carefully to minimize the dilemma. The goal is that an item could be omitted only if the participant is weak in the target competency dimension. Participants must be left in no doubt about what they are supposed and obliged to do. I sometimes use the indicators of the competency dimension in wording an item to ensure that a dimension is measured. For example, 'imagination' might be the target dimension for an in-tray item, and its indicators include 'generates options' and 'evaluates options by examining the positive and negative results of them'. The instructions for the item could be embedded in a memo from the person's boss which concludes with 'Please let me have your thoughts on our options and state the pros and cons of each option.' Such wording removes any doubts about what the participant is supposed to do and about the dimension being elicited by that particular item.

Fairness. The issue of fairness concerns whether some people have a better chance than others with the exercises for some reason independent of their strength in the competency dimensions. The simplest example of the problem is in-house jargon that some participants will know and others will not. Avoiding jargon is especially important for selection exercises used with internal and external candidates. For example, the Civil Service use the word 'minute' to refer to their equivalent of a memo. Clearly 'minute' would not be understood by external candidates, and it would disadvantage them. The same goes for the various acronyms in use in all organizations. This is basic common sense.

Just as obvious, but harder to resolve, is the exercise that puts someone from a particular background or department at a major advantage. For example, an in-tray for general managers might contain a set of accountancy papers which have to be analysed and form the basis of a report. If knowledge of accountancy itself is not critical to the target job, someone with an accountancy background would be at an obvious unfair advantage. There is no quick and simple solution to this problem; the papers would have to be omitted, and replaced by new ones that are more even-handed. With a centre for external people the equivalent problem is the exercise that favours particular degree subjects or particular work experience.

A problem for internal centres is that the members of the department in which an exercise is set could be seen as having an advantage. This is especially true if the exercise is based on genuine material from that department. The problem is less acute if the centre is truly developmental. Assessors can take people's backgrounds into account, and participants will not feel so threatened by issues of fairness. On the other hand, it is particularly difficult if the centre is used for internal promotion or is partly developmental and partly selective.

The best solution is to continue to set the exercises within the organization but to make sure that the specific material is invented. For example, one of the group exercises might be set in a managers' problem-solving meeting within the organization. Each participant is from a particular department (eg premises, personnel, O&M, office technology, legal, accounts), but his or her problem is one that has been invented and can be grasped without a specialist knowledge. In the same way, the one-to-one exercise might be a subordinate appraisal meeting or a meeting with a customer, but the background papers will be made up and will not put anyone at an advantage.

Total fairness is impossible and as a goal it is self-defeating. For example, an appraisal exercise might be said to favour those who carry out appraisals every day; a customer interview favours those who interview customers as part of their job. They are advantaged, if only by feeling more comfortable with the exercise. They are on home ground. Rather than trying to eradicate totally this type of unfairness, a solution would be to give some additional experience to those with a particular disadvantage. For example, someone who has never interviewed a customer could be allowed to practise a customer interview before the centre.

A tempting way out is to set the exercise in some mythical organization. Adams (1987) recommends that assessment centres for existing staff should have exercises set outside the organization so that the scenario is equally unfamiliar for all participants. For example, it is clearly appropriate for a bank's assessment centre to have an exercise that involves interviewing a customer, but the exercise could be said to be unfair on people without experience of customer interviews (eg people who work in one of the support departments). A way out of the problem might be provided by setting the centre in some other organization. To emphasize the customer care, perhaps a hotel or store would be a good setting. The customer interview would now be between the hotel manager and a guest. The problem is that the exercise is still unfair on people with no experience of interviewing customers, and it also carries new difficulties. First, the externalized exercises force participants to rely only on their general knowledge and common sense. This makes the measurement of some of the dimensions problematic. For example, if flexibility is included in the target competency dimensions, a less imaginative participant might appear not to be flexible simply because the options for flexibility are unknown in the hotel setting. On the other hand, the participant who goes in for flights of fancy might appear very flexible. Put more generally, the external exercise means that participants can say they did not do well because they knew nothing about the setting.

The distance between the setting of the exercise and that in which the person will work also introduces a doubt about how reliable a guide the assessment centre performance will be to actual performance. This doubt seems justified, as performance at the centre will be much more a matter of making the best of an uncertain and unfamiliar world. In addition, if the centre is meant to point out people's development needs, the simulation of an actual job within the organization will have much more impact on participants than performance on an exercise in a mythical organization. Internal exercises also have more credibility and impact on assessors, and on the organization as a whole. It will be much easier for the detractors of the assessment centre initiative in a bank to ridicule an assessor's report if it is all based on performance in running a hotel.

Locating exercises outside the organization also means that role players have to rely heavily on their general knowledge and play-acting. For example, an exercise might revolve around a subordinate appraisal. Role players know a great deal about the appraisal system in their own organization, and about the human resource procedures, career opportunities etc. However, if the interview is set in another organization, role players will have to rely much more on common sense, general knowledge and extemporizing. In a similar way, setting the exercise outside the organization makes life very much harder for assessors, who will not be viewing the exercises as experts. They will have to fall back on common sense and conjecture.

Indeed, the very design of the exercises will be much harder if they are set outside the organization. If the exercises are internal, it is reasonably easy to take material that exists within the organization (eg reports, appraisal documents etc) and adapt it. For example, a subordinate appraisal exercise can use the actual appraisal form; the in-tray can be based on actual documents. This will not be possible in an external setting. In short, there is the straightforward benefit that exercise designers are on familiar ground, which is bound to make their job easier.

External exercises also prevent the centre giving a clear preview of the job and organization to participants, and this might be an important objective. Sacrificing it can lose an important recruitment by-product of the centre if it is being used for selection.

Level of difficulty. The exercises should be appropriate to the general level of intellect and experience of the participants. The average participant should not be patronized by exercises that are too easy, nor bemused by those that are too difficult. The exercises should discriminate between people, and not be so easy that everyone does well. Nor should they be so difficult that everyone does badly. In large part, this is a question of what the exercise requires from people in the time provided. Whether the level of difficulty is right will be revealed clearly when the exercises are tried out on a dry-run.

Graded responses. It is important that the exercise does not turn on one critical insight. For example, I was once involved with an analytical exercise which participants had to approach with a particular logic. If they used the correct logic, then they did well. If they did not use it, they did very badly. This carried three problems. First, the trick could be passed on; secondly, those who did not know the trick appeared equally weak; and, thirdly, people who did badly appeared weak on all the dimensions: there was nothing to mark. The exercise should draw out the full range of differences between people across all the dimensions it is measuring. It should not divide people into good and bad.

Exercise revision

The draft exercises will require honing. In some cases a major rewrite will be necessary, and in rare cases it will be obvious that an exercise's designers just did not have their hearts in the job. Having teams of designers helps prevent this problem, as hopefully at least one of the pair will do the job enthusiastically. It is also prevented by explaining carefully at the outset the amount of work involved, and by ensuring people are interested and willing to help.

The draft exercises should be reviewed against the original goals of eliciting the dimensions, being fair, being at the right level of difficulty, allowing graded responses, and being in the right format.

Eliciting dimensions. To check whether an exercise succeeds in eliciting the dimensions as planned, it is best to visualize it being completed by participants. If it is questionable whether a particular dimension is measured, it might well be possible to change the exercise to bring the dimension out. This might be achieved by making the instructions or contents of the exercise clearer and more specific. However, there will be some exercises that cannot be altered to reveal one of the original target dimensions. It will then be a matter of determining whether any of the other exercises can be adapted to measure the dimension instead.

Fairness. The exercise should be fair, as discussed earlier. If an exercise which is meant to be for widespread use clearly favours a particular background, it will have to be rewritten.

Level of difficulty. Some exercises will be too difficult or too easy. It is usually possible to simplify an exercise that is too difficult, perhaps just by cutting back on the volume of material involved. On the other hand an exercise that is too easy might have to be abandoned. A recent example from my experience was an exercise in which the participant was required to assemble and assimilate a number of different pieces of information and put them into a well-argued case to head office for additional office space. However, once the exercise was written it was clear that all the participant could be expected to do was copy out or precis the background information – or go in for flights of fancy. It was not an exercise at all really, and would only divide participants according to how much they let their imagination run riot.

Inevitably, such difficulties might only become obvious once the exercise is written, and a new exercise has to be found. However, it is preferable not to lose the designers' goodwill by abandoning the exercise completely. In the office space example, I made the exercise into an in-tray item, so the designer was not left feeling his time had been completely wasted, or that he had failed.

Graded responses. The exercise should not turn on a single insight that is the difference between doing very well and failing very badly. An exercise with this problem might well prove hard to salvage.

Format. Some exercises might have been written as tests. In the assessment centre, the objective is to write the exercise as if it is a live issue or case. Examination-type exercises will need to be translated into the case-study format.

Harmonizing the exercises
Once they have been drafted, the co-ordinator will need to produce the exercises as a suite, and standardize the presentation of instructions, typeface etc so that the end result is professional. Standardization of the format of opening instructions will cover the timing of the exercise and the number of sections. The instructions should be clear and tell participants exactly what the setting is, and what they are meant to do. An example from an in-tray is contained in Figure 12, page 82.

Integrating the exercises
Aside from harmonizing the exercises, they can be linked together in an integrated assessment centre. One form that the integration might take is to get the participant always to assume that he or she is the same fictional character (eg a particular manager). There might be some issues that are common across the exercises. For example, I have recently produced an exercise for a bank which features a manager who has taken charge temporarily of one of the branches. It transpires from the customer one-to-one and the subordinate one-to-one that the branch used to be managed badly, and that the Assistant Manager has various weaknesses. The in-tray comes after these two exercises, and includes the participant having to write a brief report to the General Manager about the state of the branch. The report needs to include information gleaned from the earlier exercises.

Integration helps convey realism to the assessment centre. It replicates the manager going about the various settings that will normally be encountered. The risk, however, is that the linkages mean that somebody who has done badly on one exercise automatically stands to do less well on later exercises. If this happens, it makes the later exercises redundant.

Integration of exercises can be a bonus but it is by no means essential: the centre should not be distorted around this goal. Indeed integration can be a disadvantage if the centre is measuring generic management skills across the organization. In these circumstances, it might well be advisable to include a broad sweep of departments and settings to make up the exercises. That will be better both as a good simulation and politically in terms of the centre's widespread acceptability.

Figure 12
Example of in-tray instructions

In-Tray Exercise

Instructions

1. Time limit: ONE hour 30 minutes

2. Your stationery consists of:
   - company headed paper
   - company memo paper
   - plain A4 paper for reports
   - fax transmission paper
   - a pad of forms for writing outgoing telephone messages – the messages you would make if you had a telephone available.

3. Please use a separate sheet of paper for your response to each item and write:
   - the item number
   - your response to the item. Your response might be:

     a memo or letter. In this case you must write out the memo or letter itself. You should not just say you intend to write it.

     a telephone call. In this case you must indicate the points you would wish to make in the call.

     a fax. In this case you should write out the fax ready for transmission.

     a decision to delegate the item or leave it until later. If you delegate an item you must give clear instructions to the person to whom you are delegating on how you wish him or her to handle it. We want to find out how you would tackle the items so that we can get a complete view of your strengths. This is not a test of the amount you can delegate.

4. Although the exercise deals with fictitious people and events, you should refer, where appropriate, to actual people and events in this organization and elsewhere.

Background

Today is Tuesday 4 January, and it is 8.45am. Your name is Jon Chandler. You are Manager of the Edinburgh office, which employs 25 people as shown on the attached organization chart.

You have been away from the office since Christmas Eve, on holiday in Australia. You only got back last night, and have had no contact with anyone from the office since the start of your holiday. You left your Assistant Manager, Helen Palmer, in charge during your absence. The Christmas period is normally quiet, and you consider Helen a very capable person.

The attached is the in-tray that greets you on your arrival. A messenger calls by your office every half hour from 9.00am to collect outgoing mail, faxes, and messages, and to make deliveries of post and messages.

Trial of exercises

The co-ordinator should take the original designers through any modifications that he or she has made so that they still feel ownership of the exercise. The exercises are then ready to be tried out on a group of people who are at the same level in the organization as the people who will go through the centre. The group should be made up of a mix of people in terms of performance. The size of the trial group will be dictated by the number of people for which the group exercise is designed.

The trial day should start with the co-ordinator stressing that it is a test of the exercises and not of the trial group. It should be made clear that their views and comments are wanted. The trial of each exercise should concentrate particularly on:

- whether the instructions are clear
- whether the time-limit on the exercise is right. The exercises should all be run for their stated times, so that an idea is obtained of the realism of the time-limits.
- whether it is at the right level of difficulty.

The trial run of the group and one-to-one exercises should be videotaped. The recording is essential for assessor training. In making videos of group exercises, I have found it best to zoom in on two participants, who will be the ones assessors concentrate on in practising their observation and recording skills. These two people should be chosen as likely to differ in their levels of competence. At least one person should be expected to do a reasonable amount of talking during the exercise. Both should speak clearly so that assessors will be able to practise making notes from the videotape.

Timetable for the trial

It is best to test out one of the group exercises first, as it will act as an ice-breaker. The trial can then move to the one-to-one exercises. I usually run through each of these exercises twice, making video recordings. Role players will be needed for these exercises. An obvious choice is the exercise designers, as they are closest to the exercise, and it will involve them in the trial process. Next, there are the written exercises. If there are two written exercises, it is sufficient to have half of the trial group doing one and half doing the other. Finally, a second group exercise can be tried out, again making sure that it is videotaped. Whatever the precise timetable, the trial will usually be accomplished in a day. It is important to take good notes of any problems that are evident in the exercises, and a little time should be left after each one for a discussion with the designers and the trial group.

Final revision
The main discussion with designers will be on subsequent days. The co-ordinator should meet each pair of designers for about two hours (less might be needed) to discuss the trial, and changes that will be beneficial. This should be the time to put the finishing touches to the exercises and to get them ready for the assessor training. In their final version, it is very helpful to use a colour coding to distinguish between papers for participants, role players and assessors.

Marking guides

Once the exercises have been designed, it is necessary to decide upon any marking guides that will be used for assessor training. My view is that anything too detailed is a hostage to fortune because one can never anticipate all the possible responses to an exercise. I prefer to ensure that assessors really understand the competency dimensions and the behavioural indicators so that they can interpret the actual behaviour of participants in terms of the dimensions, whether or not it might have been anticipated in a marking guide. For example, with a one-to-one exercise, it is impossible to cover every possible way the conversation might unfold. It is better to make sure that the assessors can correctly classify and rate whatever actually transpires.

Some exercise designers advocate producing a 'behavioural framework' for each exercise. These frameworks contain the positive and negative behaviours that participants might produce for each competency in a given exercise. The difficulty is that some assessors lapse into using these as 'tick sheets', and this involves a risk of any unanticipated behaviours being unnoticed.

Similar arguments apply to model answers to written exercises. For example, an in-tray might contain a letter from a complaining customer. A model answer carries the danger that assessors will downgrade an equally acceptable but unanticipated alternative to the model. Indeed, the risk is that assessors become so tied to the model answer that they will overlook a brilliant answer.

However, with written exercises, it is a very good idea to indicate to assessors the dimensions that each part of the exercise is targeting. For example, each in-tray item should be focused on one or more dimensions, and these should be made clear to assessors. This is a good discipline anyway, as it provides a check that the dimensions are addressed properly. The assessors will be in no doubt what they are to mark for each part of the exercise.

There are also particular parts of exercises for which a model answer will be helpful. One obvious example is to give the correct answer to any computations that have to be carried out. Moreover, if the subordinate exercise includes a rough and ready report the subordinate has written, it will clearly be a good idea for assessors to have an annotated copy so that they know some of the problems in the report that the participant should spot.

My general reluctance to have model answers might appear to build a degree of unreliability into the marking. For example, it has been demonstrated by Smith and Tarpey (1987) that the more specific the guidelines to written exercises are, the greater the agreement on marking amongst assessors. This is hardly surprising and, as Smith and Tarpey note, the danger with highly specific guides is that assessors cease to see their input as being of value and lose their commitment to the exercise. It is an interesting dilemma, and I come down on the side of maintaining the assessors' motivation and their ability to recognize a maverick but high-quality answer.

Exercise forms

There are a number of different forms required for a centre. With the exception of observation sheets, I would advise against producing any of these forms until the exercise design is complete. It might well be that the dimensions addressed in particular exercises change during the design process. Each change will require these forms to be amended.

Observation sheets

These are simply the pro-formas on which assessors note the proceedings of one-to-one and group exercises. An example of each type of form is contained in Figures 13 and 14.

Rating forms

Rating forms are needed to accompany each of the exercises. The

Figure 13

Example of a group exercise behavioural observation and recording form

Assessor: ....

Participant A: .... Participant B: ....

Date: ....

Time	Record on participant A:	Comment	Record on participant B:

Continuation Sheet

Time	Record on participant A:	Comment	Record on participant B:

Figure 14

Example of a one-to-one exercise behavioural observation and recording form

Exercise: .... Assessor: ....

Participant: .... Date: ....

Time	Record

forms should give the positive indicators of the competency dimensions, and reproduce the rating scale. The objective is constantly to remind assessors of the scale they should be using. The forms should also have ample space for assessors to present the positive and negative evidence for the dimension. One possibility is to have a separate rating sheet for each dimension, such as the example in Figure 15 on page 90. It gives the space for evidence, and it is easy, in practice, for the administrator to make up the relevant batches of sheets for each exercise.

However, sheets for specific exercises, with several competency dimensions on each sheet, are sometimes more appropriate. After all, the detailed evidence is on observation sheets (or written out by the participants in the written exercises). Assessors are not going to fill a sheet of A4 with evidence on each dimension. An example of a rating sheet for an exercise is contained in Figure 16.

Ratings grid
A grid on which ratings can be entered as the exercises are marked is also required. This grid will be the focus for discussion at the assessors' meeting, and an example is contained in Figure 17.

Off-the-shelf and customized exercises

Off-the-shelf exercises
Using off-the-shelf exercises carries all the problems of exercises set in an external organization, together with some additional drawbacks. The most crucial is that the exercises are not specifically designed with the organization's competency dimensions in mind. That means going through the off-the-shelf catalogue and trying to choose a set of exercises that best addresses the dimensions. The obvious problem is that the competency dimensions are being fitted to the exercises rather than the other way around.

As I said in Chapter 5, it is clear that there are generic competency dimensions, and these could be measured by generic exercises. However, at present exercises usually come either with no real indication of the dimensions they measure, or with rather poorly thought-out competency dimensions. Certainly, the exercises will not properly target the tailor-made list of competency dimensions that apply to the particular job or job level of a particular organization. In future, there might well be agreement upon the generic competency dimensions, and there will be exercises designed to elicit them. There might be a

Figure 15
Example of an individual rating sheet

Sensitivity to identify others' viewpoints

Listens to others' viewpoints; adapts to other people; takes account of others' needs; sees situation from others' viewpoints; empathizes; aware of others' expectations.

Positive Evidence

Negative Evidence

Showed multiple clear evidence of a high level of competence in the dimension and no substantial negative evidence	5
Showed clear evidence of competence in the dimension and little negative evidence	4
Showed more positive evidence of competence in the dimension than negative evidence	3
Showed sufficient negative evidence to be judged lacking in competence in the dimension	2
Showed multiple clear evidence of lack of competence in the dimension and no substantial positive evidence	1

Figure 16

Example of a rating sheet for an exercise

GROUP NEGOTIATION RATING SHEET	Positive Evidence	Negative Evidence	Rating
Incisiveness to have a clear understanding Gets a clear overview of an issue; grasps information accurately; relates pieces of information; identifies causal relationships; gets to the heart of a problem; identifies the most productive lines of enquiry; appreciates all the variables affecting an issue; identifies limitations to information; adapts thinking in the light of new information; tolerates and handles conflicting/ambiguous information and ideas.			
Imagination to find ways forward Generates options; evaluates options by examining the positive and negative results if they were put into effect; anticipates effects of options on others; foresees others' reactions; demonstrates initiative and common sense.			
Self-confidence to lead the way Expresses and conveys a belief in own ability; prepared to take and support decisions; stands up to seniors; willing to take calculated risks; admits to areas of inexpertise.			
Sensitivity to identify others' viewpoints Listens to others' viewpoints; adapts to other people; takes account of others' needs; sees situation from others' viewpoints; empathizes; aware of others' expectations.			
Patience to win in the long term Sticks to a strategic plan; does not get side-tracked; sacrifices the present for the future; bides time when conditions are not favourable.			

Showed multiple clear evidence of a high level of competence in the dimension and no substantial negative evidence	5
Showed clear evidence of competence in the dimension and little negative evidence	4
Showed more positive evidence of competence in the dimension than negative evidence	3
Showed sufficient negative evidence to be judged lacking in competence in the dimension	2
Showed multiple clear evidence of lack of competence in the dimension and no substantial positive evidence	1

Figure 17

Example of a grid for ratings

Assessment Centre Grid **Name** ______________________ **Number** __________

Measure **Dimension**	Group Negotiation	Group Problem Solving	In-Tray	Analytical	Subordinate One-to-One	Interview	RESULT
Breadth of Awareness							1 2 3 4 5
Incisiveness							1 2 3 4 5
Imagination							1 2 3 4 5
Organization							1 2 3 4 5
Drive							1 2 3 4 5
Self-Confidence							1 2 3 4 5
Sensitivity							1 2 3 4 5
Co-operativeness							1 2 3 4 5
Patience							1 2 3 4 5
ASSESSOR							
FINAL RESULT							

catalogue with generic dimensions that seem about right for the job, and a set of exercises and a grid showing the relationship of the exercises to the dimensions. At present, the position is less satisfactory. The buyer must construct a grid to give some sort of match between the exercises available and the competency dimensions that must be measured.

Off-the-shelf exercises also carry the major disadvantage that they do not simulate the target job, and so they cannot be said to preview how the person would behave in the job. How people behave in the setting of the off-the-shelf exercise might be very different from how they would behave in the target job. Of course, off-the-shelf exercises might well simulate some aspects of managerial jobs that are generic across organizations. However, other aspects are likely to be missing. If assessors lapse into marking the overall quality of participants in the exercise rather than marking the specific individual dimensions, the marks will be less predictive to the extent that the exercises are not a genuine preview. The problem is exaggerated by the fact that off-the-shelf exercises can be used with little justification in terms of the job analysis. An in-tray or group exercise might be irrelevant to the target job but is included simply because most organizations have them, or because of limitations to the publisher's range of exercises.

Having off-the-shelf exercises also means that assessors come to them completely cold, having had no part in the exercise design phase. This means that they lack ownership of the exercises and they will lack an understanding of them. This will definitely make life difficult at the assessor training stage.

Furthermore, in many organizations it is thought to be wise to have parallel versions of exercises. This is particularly the case for a centre that is promotional or quasi-developmental. Parallel versions overcome the concern that the exercise might have leaked out, putting some at least at an unfair advantage. As Adams (1987) notes, parallel versions are 'infinitely easier to design when the exercise was initially tailor-made' (p 2). For example, one organization I worked with now has four versions of each exercise, with my input coming predominantly with the first set. The organization has become expert at assessment centre exercise design! If they had gone down the off-the-shelf route, they would have long since passed the point where off-the-shelf exercises would have been more expensive than the tailor-made versions.

The advantages of off-the-shelf exercises are that they can be obtained immediately, and with no development cost. In addition, there will have been some testing of the exercises, and the groundwork will have been put into their development. However, buyers should not be taken in by the notion that these exercises possess in-built psychometric properties. It is wrong to conclude that an off-the-shelf exercise carries guaranteed conformity to a normal distribution curve, as well as reliability and validity. These properties will depend on the participants and on the assessor training. Indeed, as Bray (1985), who is a pioneer in assessment centres, notes, the assessment centre method embodies a break from traditional psychometry and its elementalism.

However, off-the-shelf exercises might be a first step for an organization, perhaps combined with one or two-in-house exercises. Certainly off-the-shelf will be better than in-house versions that are badly designed for one reason or another. In particular, they might be more applicable for small organizations that cannot resource the proper development of their own exercises.

Customized exercises

A halfway stage between off-the-shelf and tailor-made exercises is customized exercises. These are supplied by consultants who take a basic exercise and customize it to the client organization. The customization must be more than simply inserting the name of the client organization on a word processor! It should give a genuine simulation of work at the job or job level in the organization, and this might mean some considerable rewriting. For example, in a subordinate appraisal one-to-one exercise, the basic character sketches of the people involved could be generic, but the actual appraisal form should be from the client organization. Similarly, the in-tray should have items that fit into the organization, and are not so generic as to be meaningless to it. Finally, for some exercises, customization is not an option. An analytical exercise with its background papers is either tailor-made or off-the-shelf. There is no halfway stage.

If customization is to be thorough it will require a good deal of work. It will be cheaper than having consultants design tailor-made exercises by themselves, but it could be more expensive than working collaboratively with consultants on exercise design.

External centres

A final option is to send people away to a centre that is run by a consultancy. For example, Skapinker (1989a) describes his experience of one such centre. On the one hand this carries the benefits of being able to 'sub-contract a time-consuming procedure, and gain the added advantage of objectivity and independence which outsiders appear to give' (Rothwell, 1985a, p 80). On the other hand, the exercises are not tailored to the organization and there will be no real sense of ownership of the process by the organization.

Nevertheless, if there are very few people to be assessed, this might be a cost-effective alternative. The centre Skapinker attended cost £1,200 for a one-day assessment plus report.

7: Non-Exercise Assessment Centre Material

The exercises are the heart of the assessment centre. However, there is a range of other material which might be included. The primary issue is the usefulness of the information that the material would provide. It is all too easy to gather information just for the sake of it. The two major uses of additional material are to add value to the assessors' meeting, and to contribute to career counselling and development planning.

If the additional information is to be useful for making decisions at the assessors' meeting, there must be an overall framework or model for combining it with the exercise information. Otherwise, there is a risk of gathering the additional information and using it in different ways depending on the participant, or not using it at all. Blinkhorn (1986) describes how an audit in one company revealed that assessors based their decisions almost exclusively on the components of the centre in which they had been involved, largely ignoring components for which they had been presented with marks, such as psychological tests and written exercises. One solution is to involve assessors in all the components of the centre. Another is to ensure that there is a framework for integrating information. This second alternative has the advantage that the additional information need only be shared with assessors after they have completed their assessments. This timing avoids the risk that they might be influenced by, and distort their ratings around, the other material.

Interviews

Many assessment centres will include one or more interviews to provide an extra measure of a subset of the competency dimensions. For example, one of the competencies might be 'breadth of awareness', which might be measured at an interview by suitable questions on current and economic affairs. The interview might also be used to try to find out about the person's drive to achieve results by asking how drive has been demonstrated in the past. Indeed, there are several competency dimensions for which the interview might be felt to give reliable information in addition to that provided by assessment centre exercises. The key is to confine the interview to measuring those competency dimensions that it is likely to measure well, and to make sure that it is carried out systematically. The dimensions and the questions should be specified beforehand; responses should be recorded and rated on the same scale that is used for the exercises.

The interview will also be used in an external centre to find out about the person's experience and qualifications. It should have been decided in advance what experience and qualifications are necessary and desirable, so that people can be assessed on these as for any other dimension.

A separate interview will also often be used at external centres for the purpose of public relations and career counselling. It would be most odd for a candidate to come to an organization and for nobody from the organization to sit down outside the context of the exercises and talk with him or her.

Self-assessment

Self-assessment will be most appropriate for a more developmental centre. Indeed, a highly developmental centre might be based largely upon self-assessment. It encourages participants to think about themselves in terms of the competency dimensions; it can reveal to them where their areas of strength and development need lie, and it can certainly be a vital preparation for the developmental feedback discussion. The self-assessment might be at the start of the centre, at its conclusion, or after each exercise.

On the other hand, self-assessment seems less appropriate for selection. People cannot be relied upon to select themselves out of a potential job, even if that would be a more rational alternative than taking a job that is unsuitable. Reilly and Chao (1982) considered self-assessment amongst various other selection procedures, and concluded from a survey of the small body of research they could find that it 'cannot be recommended as a promising alternative' (p 33).

Peer-assessment

Some centres ask participants to assess each other. This can be the basis for feedback to each other in a developmental centre.

In the case of selection, peer assessment can be useful as an additional source of information for assessors. Indeed, Reilly and Chao (1982) found it to be a good alternative selection procedure, with validities quite similar to assessment centre exercises. However, for internal candidates at a selection centre, there is a major problem of acceptability. Peer ratings could be the start of some terrible grudges.

A recent possible question mark over peer ratings comes from the evidence that people are better at peer rating those perceived as similar to themselves rather than those seen as dissimilar (Fox *et al*, 1989). This implies that the practice might discriminate against people from minorities within the group assessing each other.

Line managers' ratings

Internal centres might well include the line managers' ratings of the participant on the competency dimensions. Including line managers' ratings has the major side benefit of ensuring that they feel involved in the process. It also allows for analysis of the relationship between the ratings given by line managers and those by assessors, participants and peers.

Rating forms

If it is decided to have self, peer, or line managers' ratings, the appropriate forms will have to be designed. The precise design of these forms will depend on their uses, but they should all be targeted on the same competency dimensions that are examined in the exercises. The dimensions should be clearly defined with space given for comment. In addition, self-rating forms that are to be completed before the centre should contain a section to allow people to indicate the opportunity they have had to display the dimension in their work so far. The line manager should also be able to indicate the opportunity that the participant has had to demonstrate each competency. Both the line managers and the participants might summarize their views of the participant on each competency with a numerical rating. On the other hand, if the centre is developmental, I think that it is better not to have a numerical rating on the peer's rating form. It introduces an awkwardness into the feedback by peers, and could be used by the participant to argue with a rating given by an assessor.

Tests and inventories

The choice of whether to include any psychometric tests, personality inventories, attitude measures etc will again depend on the use to which the information is to be put. One possibility is that it will be combined with the assessment centre exercise information at the assessors' meeting. Indeed, some centres consist largely of such measures. The additional information can also be used for the feedback and career counselling and development sessions. It might help participants to reach an understanding of themselves and their performance. For example, a participant's values might not be congruent with, say, a managerial career.

A test or inventory for use at the assessors' meeting must be relevant to one or more of the target competency dimensions. This is easily and frequently lost sight of. It is felt that a measure of, say, numerical ability or of a set of personality characteristics must surely be relevant. In fact, they may have nothing to do with successful performance in the target job. The correct approach is to choose tests and inventories that measure dimensions that are expected to add to information about the competency dimensions. Ideally, these should then be checked out to determine whether people's scores in the test or inventory actually relate to performance in the competency dimensions. This is a statistical analysis which will help to confirm and refine the model of the relationship between the construct measured in the test and the competency.

A test of ability will probably be included if it is thought to measure a dimension that lies behind the competency dimension. The test dimension reveals the person's potential to acquire the competency. For example, a cognitive ability test can be seen as revealing the potential to be competent at incisiveness.

If a personality inventory is to be useful for the assessors' meeting it must also be related to the competencies. Otherwise it will be unclear how the information it provides is to be used at the meeting. For example, if one of the competencies was organization, a personality inventory might be chosen that included a dimension labelled 'planning'. The problem is that the personality information does not really add to the information from the assessment centre exercises. It is important to remember that the personality measure is actually a self-report of behaviour, and only measures a disposition inasmuch as the repetition of a particular kind of behaviour suggests that the person is disposed to behave that way. In essence, the personality inventory and assessment centre are both targeted on behaviour, and the likelihood is that the personality measure will be inferior. It is based purely on self-reported behaviour across general situations. In contrast, the assessment centre measures actual behaviour in highly relevant situations. In short, I am not certain that even a good measure of personality adds value to the assessors' meeting. It seems to me most contentious that conclusions from the exercises should be modified by information from the inventory.

If this argument is accepted, the priority will be to choose a personality measure that will be useful at the career counselling and development sessions, rather than at the assessors' meeting. The two uses of personality inventories – for the assessors' meeting and for feedback – can conflict. Thus, the assessors' meeting probably needs a straightforward measure like the 16PF or OPQ or Gordons which can be logically related and can probably be statistically related to the competency dimensions. On the other hand, participants might well feel more informed by, for example, Myers-Briggs, FIRO-B, and Schein's measure of their Career Anchors.

If an inventory is used for counselling, the feedback must be very sensitive and avoid giving the impression that the person is at the mercy of unchangeable dispositional forces. Unless feedback is done with great care, this is the message they will receive. Rightly or wrongly, the personality measure has the image of showing something enduring and not open to change, and it seems therefore to give a rather pessimistic message. Whoever carries out the feedback will need to have a good model of the relationship between the competencies and the test or inventory dimensions to be able to feed back to participants their performance on the exercises with information about their dispositions and abilities. In practice, it will usually be a job for the management development manager, rather than part of the assessor's feedback.

In-depth psychological assessment

Instead of using a simple self-completion inventory on its own, a great deal more added value might come from an in-depth assessment to find out about a person's enduring themes. It is these themes that lie behind behaviour at the assessment centre. For example, a person's lack of self-confidence might be part of a deep-seated problem. This type of information will only come from an expert assessment which will yield insights that are valuable to understanding the person's competencies, and to revealing the fundamental ways in which he or she will need to grow and develop. Indeed, it is only by understanding these themes that fundamental change is possible.

To carry out the assessment, a psychologist would need to be included amongst the assessment centre personnel. It would need to be decided if the assessment is to be used purely in counselling the individual or if a report is to be given to the assessors' meeting. I would prefer the use to be confined to the counselling session. One problem with the alternative is deciding how the psychologist's information would be combined with that from the exercises. Secondly there is the issue of the accuracy of psychologists' reports. This is less of a problem in counselling, where tentative ideas can always be amended, but it is a very real problem in assessors' meetings, which are taking decisions. The problems with individual assessments are illustrated by Ryan and Sackett (1989), who show that there is a low level of agreement between different psychologists in their assessments of the same people based on the same material.

Projective techniques

One controversial way of getting in-depth information is through the use of projective techniques (eg the Thematic Apperception Test, the Rorschach Inkblots Test and the Incomplete Sentences Blank). For example Bray (1985) describes their inclusion in the AT&T mid-career assessment centre in the Management Progress Study. He recommends considering developing projective exercises that are targeted on the organization's own dimensions rather than using the ready-made originals. However, developing such material and interpreting the results is a job that requires great expertise.

8: Getting Ready for the Centre: preselection, briefing documents and timetables

Preselection

The decision whether to have preselection will depend on the use of the centre. The arguments in favour of a valid and acceptable prescreen are that it will not only reduce the overall cost of the centre but, if the centre is for internal selection, also reduce the number of people coming away feeling they have failed. In addition, the prescreen might have an incremental validity over the assessment centre, so raising the validity of the overall process.

External selection

There will almost certainly be a system of preselection if the centre is for external selection. Depending on the numbers coming through the centre, even a small reduction via a valid prescreen will yield a saving in the overall costs of selection. However, a harsh preselection which excludes a lot of candidates carries the cost of the number of people mistakenly rejected. If there is an enormous number of applications for each vacancy, then it might be justifiable to exclude a large number (including a lot of people who would have been good) because the vacancies will still be filled with the good people that remain. On the other hand, if there are very few applicants per vacancy, the assessment centre becomes a placement centre and a harsh prescreen will not be appropriate.

The preselection is likely to be a combination of the application form and the preliminary interview. Both of these devices should be targeted on the same job-relevant dimensions that the assessment centre is examining.

The application form should be designed to elicit as much information as possible on the competency dimensions, and a system should be devised for scoring the information from the form. This does not necessarily mean going for the expensive, and often unsatisfactory, alternative of biodata. What it does mean is designing the application form around the target competencies, and then scoring it against those same dimensions.

The preselection interview should be used to sift out people who would be obvious non-starters at the assessment centre, rather than to make fine distinctions between applicants. The interview is not a fine-grade measure, and it is illogical to invite to the sophisticated assessment centre only those people who have survived the far less sophisticated interview. The interview should be given a clear focus and it should be structured so that there is not a great deal of leeway for idiosyncratic interviewers.

A cognitive test is a third possible component of the preselection system. It would have to bear a strong theoretical relationship to one or more of the assessment competency dimensions. Its use would be reinforced if there were confirmation of a strong relationship between the test and the overall assessment centre decision, or at least between the test and the assessment ratings for some competencies. Of course, this confirmation can only come after the assessment centre has been in operation. For example, in one organization's assessment centre, I found that a test of critical thinking was related strongly to the overall assessment rating. It made sense subsequently to exclude from the centre people who were clear poor performers on the test.

Internal centres

With internal centres, the question of preselection is much trickier. The main issue is whether any people in the eligible category should be prevented from attending the centre. For that matter, should all eligible people be forced to attend? The answers depend on the use of the centre. Boehm (1985) found that early identification programmes are often highly selective, whereas diagnostic and remedial programmes are usually open to all interested participants and are almost always voluntary.

The area of prescreening was reviewed by Warmke (1985), and he specifies the following possibilities:

Management nomination or recommendation. The problem with this is the motivation of the nominator, especially if the nomination is just one person acting alone and is not accompanied by any real documentation. Good people might not be nominated in case they are lost to the department or area; poor people might be recommended to teach them a lesson. These problems can be overcome by requiring that nominations are ratified, and that they are accompanied by adequate documentation.

Self-nomination. The problem here is that it might do little to reduce the overall numbers, but it is likely to be viewed favourably by participants.

Setting minimum requirements, such as tenure or performance. This is easy to administer, objective and likely to be acceptable.

Prescreening interviews. Warmke recommends these for use more as counselling sessions, in which the potential participants learn more about the job and hopefully select themselves out if it clearly is not appropriate to attend the centre.

Aptitude tests. For internal candidates, I believe the problems of acceptability must be weighed very carefully against the test's validity. If tests are used, then those who 'fail' must be counselled very carefully and sensitively.

Biodata. Biodata gained some popularity during the mid-1980s as a method of preselection. In essence, it refers to using the person's past (*bio*graphical *data*) to predict the future. It might be aspects of the past over which the person had no control (eg rural or urban upbringing) or it might deal with past behaviour, and past and present attitudes. Warmke says biodata has a favourable to neutral participant reaction. My experience is the opposite. As a client of mine once said, 'It's a pretty difficult job, telling someone they've failed the biodata.' I agree, and I do not think this lack of acceptability is outweighed by the biodata's validity. People will see biodata as an unfair method of deciding eligibility for advancement. Moreover, they will be right. Whilst biodata might have a statistical relationship with success, there will always be anomalies, and nobody wants to be the anomaly.

Peer nominations. Again, Warmke seems impressed by the potential use of peer nominations. But I would be concerned about the tensions it might generate if someone is not nominated.

Job knowledge tests. These have a good validity – perhaps because they provide an estimate of genuine motivation. However, Warmke reports their acceptability to be low. They are, in any case, more applicable to supervisory than managerial jobs.

There is no need to be confined to one prescreen. They can be used in a battery. For example, the process might start with self-nomination to exclude people who are insufficiently motivated. Self-nominations could then be submitted to a management committee to evaluate the nomination in the light of performance and experience. Then there might be a prescreen interview and tests to decide on the priorities for attendance at the assessment centre rather than as a means of excluding people.

In deciding how to prescreen, I think acceptability should be the major consideration. Of course, what is unacceptable in one company (eg administration of psychological tests) might be routine for others. However, I believe it is preferable in general to define the eligible category and then leave it to self-selection, perhaps after a counselling interview. Excluding people from the centre on the basis of a personality inventory, cognitive test or biodata form is too demotivating to be acceptable. The only grounds for exclusion must be criteria which people feel they can do something about, such as a minimum length of service or a minimum performance record.

If the centre is for development, there is little justification in excluding anyone in the eligible category from attending. If cost is the problem, it would be better to think imaginatively for a solution (eg a self-assessment centre) than to sacrifice the developmental opportunity.

Briefing documents

The second pre-centre activity to be considered in this chapter is the distribution of briefing materials. These are required for the participants and for the organization. For external candidates, the document might be no more than a page telling them what to expect. It should set the tone of the centre, and nowadays the emphasis will be on the candidate finding out about the potential employer as much as the employer finding out about the candidate. The objective is that both should reach a rational and well-informed decision. The briefing should give details of how the assessment centre is made up in terms of exercises and interviews etc, and there should be a note about the roles of the various people at the centre. It should also be clear how the decision will be reached and conveyed to candidates. Finally, of course, the document should make clear domestic details such as the time of arrival, and likely time of departure.

For internal centres, the briefing will be much more comprehensive. It needs to explain the centre and how it fits into the career system of the organization. Participants should be reminded of the purpose of the centre, especially if it is development. Steps that go before their attendance at the centre (eg manager's appraisal, application sift etc) should be described, along with what they can expect after the centre. Particular emphasis should be given to the centre's role in the training and development process if it is an internal centre. It is useful with internal centres to summarize the briefing in the form of a flow chart that shows who does what, and when.

In briefing for an internal centre, I believe that participants should be told as much as possible about the centre itself, especially the competencies. It seems wholly illogical to know the competency dimensions of success in an organization, and then to keep them a secret. It seems far better to be open and specify exactly what dimensions will be examined in the centre. In any case, the competency dimensions cannot be kept a secret for long because they will be central to the management development workshops or modules. However, there often seems to be a feeling that somehow the assessment will be contaminated if people know what they are being assessed against. This has some truth only if the measurement of the competency dimensions in the exercises is particularly gross. For example, participants at a centre with achievement motivation as a dimension must not gain points merely by parroting the words 'We must do this excellently.' The exercises must be stiff enough so that people cannot score points by mouthing platitudes.

I also think it is desirable to give the participants some foreknowledge of the exercises, at least in outline terms. They will come to learn of them anyway through their peers. Clearly it would not be sensible to go into detail, but an outline will put everyone on equal terms, and will not invalidate the centre. If there are parallel exercises, just the common denominator of the different versions could be given. For example, the briefing might say one of the exercises will require participants to tackle an in-tray that might typically be found on the desk of someone at the target level.

Aside from the briefing for participants, there needs to be a briefing document for the participant's manager. This should stress the primary purpose of the centre, especially if that purpose is developmental. It will give a very mixed message if people come back from a developmental centre and are asked by their managers whether they passed. The document must stress that it is not a pass/fail system and that participants are attending it to help their development. The briefing will need to take particular care not to appear critical of managers' abilities to rate current performance. The emphasis can often be that the centre focuses upon participants' performance in a different job from the present one.

Finally, there will need to be a briefing document for the organization as a whole, so that everyone is clear about the new system. It need not be lengthy, but it should give a brief introduction to the assessment centre process, which describes how the centre has been designed to look at participants in terms of the competency dimensions that mark out successful performers at the job or job level. It should be explained that the centre uses job simulations, and that these exercises are observed by trained people. The briefing should also explain the role of the centre in the HR system, and why it is being used. It will also need to describe who the potential participants are, and who the assessors will be.

Timetables

The final material needed before the centre can get underway is the timetable. The timetable for an assessment centre should give assessors sufficient time to complete their ratings competently after each interactive exercise. They must not get a backlog of work to be assessed. The utility of the centre will be destroyed if the assessments cannot be carried out conscientiously and if assessors cannot be given pause for thought. A rule of thumb will be to allow assessors 15 minutes to mark each participant after an interactive exercise (ie they will need 30 minutes after a group exercise and 15 minutes after each one-to-one exercise.) A certain amount of leeway can be gained by leaving the marking of written exercises until the evening if the centre is lasting more than a day.

Whilst assessors need gaps, participants, by contrast should have the minimum amount of waiting between exercises. Normally these requirements can only be reconciled by dividing the participant group and running the written exercises and tests in parallel with the one-to-one exercises and interviews.

Obviously the timetable should have a starting time that allows people to travel without being rushed; alternatively, arrangements should be made for them to stay overnight before the centre. The centre's chairperson should welcome participants and brief them as described in Chapter 9. The participants can then fill in any pre-centre self-assessment forms. Some centres also include a warm-up exercise before the assessors come into the room. This gives people a

Figure 18

Example of an assessment centre timetable

Day 1

10.30	assemble and coffee
11.00–11.15	welcome and introduction
11.15–12.15	complete pre-assessment centre questionnaire
12.15–13.00	warm-up exercise
13.00–14.00	lunch
14.00–14.15	managers' meeting – preparation
14.15–15.15	managers' meeting – discussion
15.15–15.30	managers' meeting – write-up
15.30–15.50	tea
15.50–17.20	analytical written exercise (participants 1, 2 & 3)
15.50–17.00	subordinate 1:1 (participants 4, 5 & 6)
15.50–16.10	prepare
16.10–16.40	role play
16.40–17.00	write-up
17.30–19.00	analytical written exercise (participants 4, 5 & 6)
17.50–19.00	subordinate 1:1 (participants 1, 2 & 3)
17.50–18.10	prepare
18.10–18.40	role play
18.40–19.00	write-up

Day 2

08.30–08.45	group negotiation – prepare
08.45–09.45	group negotiation – discussion
09.45–10.15	coffee
10.15–11.45	in-tray
11.55–12.25	interview (participants 1, 2 & 3)
12.35–13.05	interview (participants 4, 5 & 6)
13.05–13.30	debrief on assessment centre with administrator
13.30	lunch and participants depart
15.00–19.00	assessors' meeting

Figure 19
Example of Assessor 1's timetable

Day 1		Room	Participant
14.15–15.15	observe managers' meeting group discussion exercise	D	1 and 4
15.15–16.10	mark discussion exercise		1 and 4
16.10–16.40	observe subordinate 1:1	B	5
17.00–18.10	mark subordinate 1:1		5
18.10–18.40	observe subordinate 1:1	B	2
Evening	mark subordinate 1:1		2
Evening	mark analytical exercises		3 and 6
Day 2			
08.45–09.45	observe group negotiation	D	2 and 5
09.45–11.55	mark group negotiation		2 and 5
11.55–12.25	interview	B	1
12.35–13.05	interview	B	4
13.00–13.30	mark interviews		
13.30–14.30	mark in-trays		
15.00–19.00	assessors' meeting	D	

chance to settle and get used to the sound of their own voices. The centre itself should preferably start with a group exercise to settle people down further. Then it should move on to the written exercises and one-to-one exercises. Preferably, each participant should be allocated a number to identify his or her written answers. These numbers will only be known to the collator of marks so that assessors mark these exercises blind of the impressions they have reached from the interactive exercises. An example of a timetable that gives assessors some leeway, but which keeps candidates or participants occupied is given in Figure 18.

Each assessor and participant should be given a personal customized timetable derived from the master timetable. The timetable should show the room the person is in, and the activity. Examples of an assessor's and a participant's timetable derived from the above master timetable are shown in Figures 19 and 20.

Figure 20
Example of Participant 1's timetable

Day 1		Room	Assessor
10.30	assemble	D	
11.00–11.15	welcome and introduction	D	
11.15–12.15	complete pre-assessment centre questionnaire	D	
12.15–13.00	warm-up exercise	D	
13.00–14.00	lunch		
14.00–15.30	managers' meeting group exercise	D	I
14.00–14.15	managers' meeting – preparation		
14.15–15.15	managers' meeting – discussion		
15.15–15.30	managers' meeting – write-up		
15.30–15.50	tea		
15.50–17.20	analytical exercise	D	II
17.50–19.00	subordinate 1:1	A	III
17.50–18.10	preparation		
18.10–18.40	role playing		
18.40–19.00	write-up		

Day 2		Room	Assessor
8.30–09.45	group negotiation meeting	D	II
08.30–08.45	prepare		
08.45–09.45	group meeting		
09.45–10.15	coffee		
10.15–11.45	in-tray	D	III
11.55–12.25	interview	B	I
13.05–13.30	debrief on assessment centre		
13.30	lunch and depart		

9: Assessment Centre Personnel

The assessors

The assessors' group will include people who have helped with the exercise design. They will have gained understanding and commitment to the assessment centre process. If there are six exercises, and teams of two designers, then there are already twelve potential assessors. However, the group might need to be broadened to make sure that there are enough assessors to cope with the volume of participants or to include in the assessors' panel all the departments and interest groups in the organization. Often, for political reasons, organizations have more trained assessors than are strictly required by the number of participants. A convenient time for including more people is when parallel exercises are developed. Another six people can be brought into the panel, each working alongside one of the experienced assessors.

The number of assessors who must be trained in the first training courses depends on the number of participants who will go through the initial centres, and the ratio of assessors to participants at each centre. Group exercises should always be observed in a ratio of 1:2, as an assessor cannot be expected to follow more than two participants. Even with this restriction, it is still possible to timetable a batch of 12 participants, and split them into two groups of six for the group exercises, making a 1:4 ratio for the centre as a whole. The groups would run sequentially, with the same three assessors acting as observers.

If the 1:2 ratio is used initially at least, and if there will be 60 participants in the first year, it can be seen that 15 assessors will be needed, on the assumption that each of them assesses twice a year, which is about the minimum to keep in practice.

Generally, it is better for line managers to be in the majority as assessors. Using line managers ensures that they own the process and do not see it as the property of the HR department. However, the extent to which this is an issue depends on the organization, and certainly, there might be a disproportionate number of assessors from HR without the rest of the organization feeling that it has lost ownership. Aside from line managers and people from the HR department, it is also possible to have expert assessors from outside the organization. Gaugler *et al* (1987) found that assessment centres were more predictive of performance when the assessors were psychologists than when they were managers. This might be used as a reason to replace line managers, but I think that the loss in terms of involvement and commitment will be unacceptable. As Greatrex and Phillips (1989) observe, for BP 'the lack of expert assessors is traded off against the high ownership of senior management for the programme and its high face validity with participants' (p 39).

The assessment centre might still include an external expert, but to do a different job from the exercise assessors. The expert's role might be to find out about the enduring themes that underlie a person's life, as described in Chapter 7. For example, the Civil Service Selection Boards include a psychologist and they find this person's insights and independent view of considerable value. Nevertheless, using a private-sector consultant will add considerably to the costs of the centre, and his or her presence must not take undue emphasis away from the simulation exercises. It could also be demotivating for the line assessors who might feel they must bow to the expert.

There should be no problem in getting line managers to serve as assessors if the groundwork has been laid correctly. First, the process will hopefully have top-level endorsement. If it is driven from the top, line managers will be more willing than if it appears that they are doing a favour for an HR department scheme. Secondly, the system should have been sold to the line managers by involving them from the outset. Potential assessors should have been included in the job analysis interviews, and then involved in one of the exercises. Most likely, they will then want to see the process through and act as assessors. After all, by this stage, they will be convinced of the utility of the assessment centre.

The level of the assessors in the organization is important. If the process is to be seen as credible they must be senior to the participants. The usual advice is for them to be two levels senior, although this will, of course, depend on the detailed structuring of the organization. If the centre is looking at long-term potential, assessors should be from the level upon which the centre is targeted. There will be a distinct credibility problem if future senior managers are chosen by middle managers, just as there would be a problem if people on the shop-floor assessed people's supervisory skills.

Equally, it is possible to err in the direction of having assessors who are too senior. I know one large organization whose managing director proposes to act as an assessor for their fast-track centre. This is excellent from the point of view of top-level endorsement and commitment. My reservations are whether he will bow to other assessors' opinions, or at least whether they will feel able to argue their points of view; whether he will have the time to be trained properly; and whether his presence will make the process unnecessarily daunting for participants.

The chairperson

The chairing role is normally taken by a person from the management development function. The level of the chairperson will depend on the centre. Often it will be appropriate for the management development manager to be the chairperson. However, a junior management centre might be chaired by someone of lower status, and a senior management or directors' centre might be chaired by a director. If there are a lot of centres each year, the chair might be delegated during the running of the centre, with the manager arriving for the assessors' meeting. Indeed, in some large organizations, assessment is a round-the-year activity, and the management development manager cannot always be present even at the assessors' meetings. In such cases an equally credible chairperson must be found. It might be someone who is carrying out the role full time on secondment. The full-time nature of the role gives them a credibility and authority they otherwise might not have.

The function of the chairperson during the centre is to ensure its smooth and fair running. It is essentially a job of quality control, and involves overseeing the participants, the assessors, and the role players. The function at the assessors' meeting is both to chair the meeting and to hear at first hand the assessors' comments on participants.

Overseeing the participants

Participants should be well briefed, not suffer unnecessarily from stress, and approach each exercise with a fresh mind. To help achieve this the chairperson should brief participants on their arrival. The briefing needs to remind them of a number of points which will also have been mentioned in the pre-centre written briefing, and should deal particularly with what they can expect during the centre. They should be made familiar with the timetable, and reminded that each person is responsible for being in the right place at the right time. The exercises should be described very briefly to ensure that everyone has an understanding of the different types of exercise.

The ground rules at the centre should also be laid down. These will include a request that once the day is underway participants should not talk to each other about the exercises. The timetables are individual and some people may not yet have done an exercise that others have just finished. Finally the chairperson must stress that participants are not in competition with each other, but are being assessed against general standards.

During the centre, the chairperson is a point of reference for participants if they have any problems. In particular, he or she will need to deal with anyone who is suffering from stress, becoming unduly despondent, or reacting very negatively to the centre. Finally, at the end of the centre it is a good idea to spend at least some time with participants in a debriefing session. They can give their views on the centre, and clear up any doubts or anxieties.

Overseeing the assessors

A second key role for the chairperson during the centre relates to the assessors. The validity and reliability of the assessment centre process rests on the assessors' abilities in the three key areas of observing and recording participants' behaviour; categorizing behaviour; and rating behaviour. To ensure that standards are met, the chairperson should be satisfied that assessors are taking full observation notes. There should also be an alertness to whether assessors are using the behavioural criteria to categorize their responses, and whether they are rating each competency dimension using the scale properly and independently of the other competency dimensions. In practice, problems with categorizing and rating are more likely to become evident at the assessors' meeting than during the centre.

The chairperson should also make sure that assessors do not talk to each other about the participants they have been observing until the assessors' meeting at the end of the centre. Such talk may well influence the assessors of subsequent exercises. Assessors should also not share information with participants before the feedback meeting.

Overseeing the role players

Finally, the chairperson must monitor the role players as far as possible. Feedback on the role plays will come from assessors and participants, and any obvious problems in the role plays must be discussed.

Role players

As Rodger and Mabey (1987) remark, the key contra-indicator for a role player is an interest in amateur dramatics. People are needed who will play the parts in an undramatic way. One possible source of people for role playing is the training department, but it can also be a useful way of bringing new people into the assessment centre system who will go on to become assessors. I try to keep down the number of people involved in the role plays at any one time. If there is a choice between using a small number of role players frequently for a short period and then phasing in a new group or using a large number infrequently, then I would go for the small number. They can then become 'experts' at their roles.

Role players will need to be thoroughly familiar with the briefs, and I have found it helpful to have a one-day meeting with the group of role players to resolve any doubts and ambiguities in the parts they are to play. This is best done after the trial and videoing of the one-to-one exercises. The role players should then practise the roles amongst themselves, and keep a record of any points that arise.

The starting point for the role playing is the brief that the exercise designers have written. The role player meetings will then put extra detail on this brief. By the time of the centre, all the role players should approach the roles as far as possible in the same way. What role players must establish is their general approach to the exercise and their answers to key questions that might be asked by participants. At the centre itself each role player should act in a similar manner with each participant, for example by giving the same information to each participant in response to the same question. The aim is to provide a standardized backdrop against which each participant's competencies can be demonstrated. However, the role can never be scripted, as it is most important that the interaction with the participant is natural.

Role players should not be obstructive by keeping information hidden when a participant is asking directly about a particular area. However, neither should they volunteer information to the participants too readily. Participants are required to elicit information and to identify a logical approach to a problem. Information should only be volunteered if the participant is unable to direct the discussion. In such cases, volunteering is helpful to avoid participants feeling that they have failed the exercise completely. Detailed guidelines on when to volunteer information should be agreed and included in the role players' brief. For example, it might say 'If, after ten minutes the participant appears to be getting nowhere, start to volunteer information. Do not, however, do this too soon.'

Apart from the initial meetings, role players should also feed in any points that arise during the playing of the roles with participants. It is also a good idea to have occasional meetings – say every six months – amongst role players to update, collate and implement any enhancements to playing the role.

A concern that some people voice about role plays is whether they are unfair. It is argued that, because of their interactive nature, no two participants face the same stimulus. Of course, this is true at a micro level, but the role player training is aimed at ensuring that participants receive a similar stimulus at a broader level. The theme of the part of the role player is standardized, even if the precise words are not. The argument about standardization can be applied to any assessment other than a written exercise administered under perfectly controlled conditions. The answer is to go for a level of standardization that does not destroy the basis of the exercise.

The administrator

A capable administrator is the key to the successful running of the centre. It is vital to have someone bright and energetic who can get on top of the co-ordinating activities of the centre. He or she must also, of course, be able to handle confidential information.

The administrator should be in charge of all the preparation for the centre, including getting the materials ready, corresponding with assessors, role players and participants, and arranging accommodation. All this work is done before the centre. It will not be necessary for the administrator to be in full-time attendance at the centre itself, once it has been running a couple of times and any problems have been ironed out. Once the centre is running smoothly, there will be long gaps during the exercises with the administrator having nothing to do. Instead of the administrator, the chairperson can start and stop the exercises. It sounds uneconomic to have the expensive chairperson doing the administration at the centre, but he or she must be there anyway.

Checklists for running the centre

Working through the running of the centre chronologically, the following is the major checklist. Many of these matters will fall to the administrator.

Well before the centre

- Assessors and role players must be informed in plenty of time that they are being asked to take part in the centre.
- Invitations must be sent to the participants, together with briefing documents.
- Briefing documents must also be sent to participants' managers, if the centre is internal. If there are managers' rating forms, they must also be sent out.
- Accommodation for the centre must be booked.

Shortly before the centre
Having got everyone and everything booked, there is a checklist of materials for the centre itself. The centre's administrator needs to ensure that sufficient numbers of the following obvious and less obvious items are all ready for the start of the centre:

- exercises, marking guides and role players' briefs
- answer paper/booklets
- observation sheets, rating sheets and marking grids
- clip-boards for assessors when observing
- psychometric test material
- self-assessment sheets
- end of assessment centre evaluation sheets
- pens, pencils, pencil sharpeners and erasers
- paper clips, stapler
- individual timetables for assessors and participants
- name badges/table place labels
- labels for room doors
- calculators
- flip-chart paper and pens.

Of course some of these will not be relevant to a particular centre, and there will be other specific things which must be included. The overall message is to make an inventory and make sure that all the materials are despatched to the centre.

On the day

During the centre, there should be no need for a checklist if all the preparation has been carried out. The most important thing is to make sure that timetables are adhered to. Otherwise the centre will get out of synchronization. The chairperson will also have to sort out any unlikely emergency, such as someone suffering from the stress of the occasion.

Accommodation for the centre

The minimum space for a centre with six participants is:

- assessors' administrator's office
- participants' relaxing room
- one large room for group and written exercises
- three small rooms for one-to-one exercises, and interviews if applicable.

Hotels are often used for centres, but this amount of space will clearly add up to quite a large bill. On top of the cost for the assessment rooms, meal and extras, comes the cost of accommodation for assessors, participants, and the chairperson. Furthermore, care should be taken with the sort of work rooms the hotel is offering. A set of converted bedrooms at an airport hotel can be a rather unexciting prospect. It is preferable to get a private annexe or wing. However, such space is in short supply, and will need to be booked well in advance. The hotel should also be flexible about meal times to allow assessors to get on with their marking in the evening and to eat when they want.

Despite its expense, I think it is preferable to hold centres for internal people away from the organization's normal premises. It avoids interruptions, and helps the psychological immersion in the centre's activities. Certainly, if it is to be held within the organization, a space that is private is required, such as a training centre.

10: Assessing the Participants

Observing and recording the exercises

In the group exercises the assessors observe two participants in a room laid out approximately as shown in Figure 21. Assessors must make a reasonably detailed record of what their participants do and say. An assessor may also note down significant actions and contributions by other participants which could account for their own participants' behaviour. For example, another participant might be extremely rude to one of the participants being assessed. The assessors should record these contextual events in the column marked 'comments' on the observation sheet (see Figure 13, page 86).

Figure 21
Layout of room for group exercise

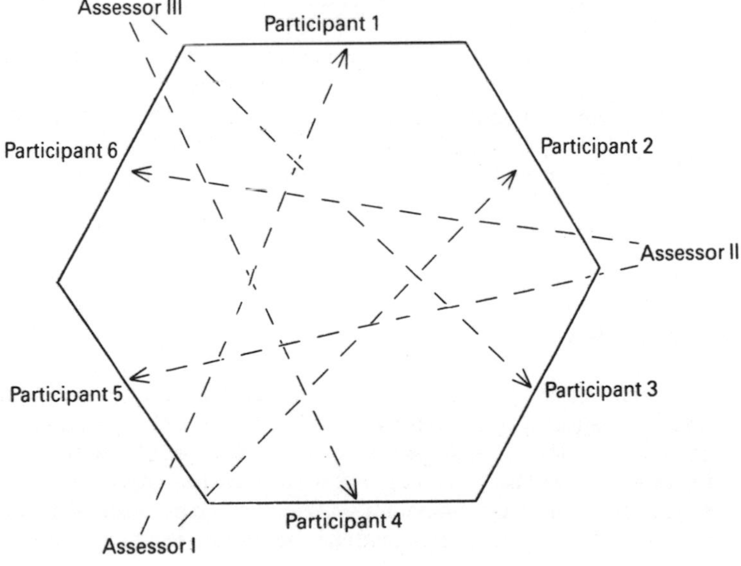

In the one-to-one exercises, the assessor is alone in the room with the participant and the role player. The assessor should record the participant's behaviour, but again might make the occasional note of what the role player did and said.

In the written exercises, the observing and recording is, of course, done by the participant. However, if there is a debriefing session after a written exercise, the assessor will again need to record the participant's comments.

Classifying behaviour

In the group and one-to-one exercises (the interactive exercises), the assessors must classify the recorded behaviour under the competency dimensions that are being assessed. They should not feel the need to classify every piece of behaviour under one or other dimension. It might well be that a particular piece of behaviour is an instance of none of the competency dimensions being assessed. Equally, it is possible that a particular observation covers more than one competency dimension. For example, 'puts forward an accurate summary of the other person's views' will be positive evidence of both incisiveness and sensitivity. However, even in this example it is possible to separate the evidence on incisiveness (the accurate summary) from the sensitivity (the other person's views). It is good discipline if assessors try not to double-classify their observations, but make a decision under which dimension the behaviour is to be classified. Classifications are best made whilst the exercise is in progress, with a margin note, such as 'in +' for a positive example of incisiveness.

In the written exercises, classification is easier. Assessors have a guide to the dimensions that different parts of the exercise are addressing, and they have time to reflect on and consider their classification.

Rating behaviour

At the end of the exercise, and only at the end, assessors should bring together a summary of their classified observations for each competency dimension on the rating sheets. They should separate their positive and negative evidence for each of the dimensions. They must then summarize the balance of evidence by assigning a rating to the dimension, using a scale such as the one on the next page.

Showed multiple clear evidence of a high level of competence in the dimension and no substantial negative evidence	5
Showed clear evidence of competence in the dimension and little negative evidence	4
Showed more positive evidence of competence in the dimension than negative evidence	3
Showed sufficient negative evidence to be judged lacking in competence in the dimension	2
Showed multiple clear evidence of lack of competence in the dimension and no substantial positive evidence	1

The scale does not ask for a simple count of the instances of positive and negative evidence. It asks assessors to weigh both the quality and the quantity of evidence, and to make a judgement. The judgemental nature of the assessment is inevitable, and is one reason for having highly paid assessors to do the task.

It is important that all assessors abide by the rating scale as defined, so that two assessors mean the same thing by a given rating. Assessors must also be encouraged to use the whole of the rating scale. The wording of the high and low points is deliberately not at the absolute extremes of competence. If they were worded with more extremity, they would be used so rarely as effectively to be redundant.

Sins of omission and commission

In making their ratings, assessors come across the vexed issue of sins of omission and commission. The problem is clearest in interactive exercises when participants give no evidence that can be noted down for one of the more cognitive dimensions that are meant to be measured. For example, suppose that breadth of awareness is a competency dimension being measured in a group exercise, and someone has shown no breadth at all, but neither has he or she shown an actual muddled ignorance of the world. The omission will not appear under the observation notes, whereas referring to the 'nine countries of the EC' would have appeared as an observation note. What happens when assessors fill out the rating sheet? Do they put 'said nothing to show breadth' as negative evidence, in just the same way that they would note the EC mistake? The same issue arises with the written exercises if an item is left out. For example, if a report is not written in an in-tray exercise, does that count as negative evidence for the target dimensions of the omitted item?

The ambiguity can lead to assessors feeling that they have insufficient evidence to make a rating for a dimension. There is nothing positive under the competency dimension, but there are no negative observations either. In practice, if assessors cannot have any faith in their rating, it is better to give a 'not rated' than a 3, which will be misleading at the assessors' meeting. However, if assessors are unable to make ratings, it is most likely to be because they cannot take as negative evidence the failure to display the competency dimension. The exercises should be designed and administered, so that these ambiguities do not arise. The design and administration of the exercises should be such that the fact that there is no evidence can itself be counted as negative evidence. The design of the exercise must demand the demonstration of the target competency dimensions, rather than allowing it to be optional; and the administration of the exercise must give the participant every opportunity to display the dimension. This is where the light-touch chairing of group exercises is important. For example, if each participant is gently drawn into the group discussion and given the opportunity to show breadth, then someone who still shows no breadth can be assumed to be lacking in this competency dimension, rather than to be shy. With written exercises, the instructions must be clear, and, as a final measure, there can be a quick interview at the end of the in-tray to cover any omitted items. If it is not possible to build in a target competency to an exercise satisfactorily, it is better that the dimension is not examined in that exercise.

Judgement is important with sins of omission. Clearly, people cannot have stacked against them the infinity of things they might have said or done. It is up to the assessors to note major omissions, and up to the exercise designers to ensure that such omissions are unambiguous.

Timing of ratings

I have said that ratings should be made after each exercise. In fact, there is a choice. The AT&T approach is to rate at the end of all the exercises, and Dobson and Williams (1989) reported that the same approach is used by the British army's Regular Commissions Board. This seems at odds with what we know about information decay, and I cannot really see the arguments in its favour.

Rating by exercise
I have also concentrated upon rating each competency dimension separately. Another possibility is to rate each exercise as a whole with an overall mark, or to rate each of the outputs or roles in an exercise. However, if there is to be feedback, the competency dimension ratings should not be replaced by the overall exercise rating or ratings in terms of outputs or roles. People need to be told what they should do to perform better, and this feedback must be in terms of the competencies. For example, if someone does badly in the business development role on the customer one-to-one exercise, the poor performance must be fed back in terms of the need to develop competencies such as listening skills. Furthermore, I cannot see how either the overall mark or the marks for the roles can be other than mediated by the dimensions. Certainly, assessors cannot mark successfully by exercise and by competency dimension at the same time. Marking by exercise will serve only to encourage the halo effect across dimensions. If an overall mark for the exercise is wanted for some reason, I think it should be calculated simply as the mean of the dimension ratings, rather than something upon which assessors focus their attention.

The assessors' meeting

Once the exercises are completed, the assessors must finish off their assessments. These should be handed in to the chairperson or administrator, who will be collating marks by filling in a grid. The end result will be a grid that has been completed, such as that in Figure 22. Each grid should be photocopied for each assessor and for the chairperson, and the assessors' meeting can then be held.

Until the assessors' meeting, assessors will have observed and rated behaviour independently of each other across the various exercises. At the meeting, assessors will share these ratings and the behavioural examples in order to come to a common view of participants in each competency, particularly a view on each participant's strengths and development needs. They will also probably make recommendations on each participant's career development. The focus of the meeting is the observed behaviour in the exercises at the centre. Anecdotal information collected outside the assessment day must not be introduced. For example, an assessor may have met one of the participants and have private views on that person. These views must be kept private.

The procedure for the meeting is to take one participant at a time

Figure 22

Example of a completed grid for ratings

Assessment Centre Grid **Name** Ruth Naylor **Number** 03

Measure / **Dimension**	Group Negotiation	Group Problem Solving	In-Tray	Analytical	Subordinate One-to-One	Interview	RESULT
Breadth of Awareness		5	3	4		5	1 2 3 4 5
Incisiveness	4	3	4	3			1 2 3 4 5
Imagination	2		3	3	4		1 2 3 4 5
Organization		3	1	2	2		1 2 3 4 5
Drive		4	3		5	4	1 2 3 4 5
Self-Confidence	5	4	3		4		1 2 3 4 5
Sensitivity	2		3	3	2		1 2 3 4 5
Co-operativeness		1	3		2	1	1 2 3 4 5
Patience	4		4	3		3	1 2 3 4 5
ASSESSOR	NM	JLV	CMC	JLV	CMC	NM	
FINAL RESULT							

Figure 23

Example of a completed grid for ratings and resolved profile

Assessment Centre Grid **Name** Ruth Naylor **Number** 03

Measure / **Dimension**	Group Negotiation	Group Problem Solving	In-Tray	Analytical	Subordinate One-to-One	Interview	RESULT
Breadth of Awareness		5	3	4		5	1 2 3 (4) 5
Incisiveness	4	3	4	3			1 2 (3) 4 5
Imagination	2		3	3	4		1 2 (3) 4 5
Organization		3	1	2	2		1 (2) 3 4 5
Drive		4	3		5	4	1 2 3 4 (5)
Self-Confidence	5	4	3		4		1 2 3 (4) 5
Sensitivity	2		3	3	2		1 (2) 3 4 5
Co-operativeness		1	3		2	1	1 (2) 3 4 5
Patience	4		4	3		3	1 2 3 (4) 5
ASSESSOR	NM	JLV	CMC	JLV	CMC	NM	
FINAL RESULT							

and to go through the competencies in turn. For each competency, the chairperson reads out the ratings. If there is a discrepancy amongst the ratings, the chairperson asks for behavioural examples from the different exercises. Once information on all the exercises measuring the competency has been shared, it is considered by assessors, who must produce an overall rating on the competency. Minor discrepancies of just one point are usually resolved easily. Larger discrepancies might take some time if the centre is for promotion and assessors have to be satisfied about the accuracy of the resolved rating.

Once all the competencies have been dealt with, the assessors will have a profile in front of them, such as that in Figure 23. They will agree clear strengths and development needs, which will be fed back to the participant. If it is a promotion centre, they must also arrive at a recommendation on the person's promotion and career development. This comes from reviewing the overall profile, together with the person's apparent strengths and limitations. It will need to have been agreed whether there is any weighting to be applied to the competency dimensions, or whether all are to be regarded as equal. Assessors will also need some advice on the ease of overcoming limitations in the different dimensions. A weakness is a bigger problem in a less improvable dimension than in a readily improvable one. They will also be able to make use of any available information on potential as shown by tests and inventories or by the in-depth psychological report.

The meeting for a centre that involves internal people who are being assessed for promotion or for a fast track is the most difficult and lengthy. The centre places a heavy responsibility on assessors, and they could easily need an hour for some participants. (Indeed, Deloitte Haskins and Sells are reported to spend 1.5 hours per individual, Stevens, 1985.) They will need this if only to feel satisfied that they have done justice to each participant. The slowness comes from the time needed to compare evidence in arriving at an overall rating for each competency dimension, and in weighing the profile to make a decision. I would not advise trying to shorten this process. It is important that the assessors feel they have done a thorough job and that they are comfortable with their decision.

The length of the meeting will be increased if it is intended to compile a report on each person at the meeting. I do not see the need for this. It seems more sensible to nominate before the meeting the assessors who will give the feedback to each participant. These people will be responsible for writing reports after the meeting, for which they will be given the rating sheets of their fellow-assessors at the end of the meeting. It is better to do this and give the participant the fullest possible feedback, rather than to write brief reports at the centre which consist of only a couple of rushed lines for each competency dimension.

External selection meetings are much shorter than those for internal promotion. There is less feeling of onerous responsibility, and assessors might well scan the marks for each dimension and, if there is an obvious resolution, agree it speedily and move to the next dimension. Assessors will only describe their comments for individual exercises for discrepancies that are harder to resolve. Usually the meeting can go through each person in 15 minutes. There is no real need to write an integrated report on each person. Once the profile has been agreed in external selection centres, it will probably be sufficient to collect assessors' rating sheets and attach these to the marking grid and profile.

When the centre is to be used purely for development, the assessors' meeting will also be reasonably straightforward. Assessors will need to agree their ratings for the competency dimensions, and point out what they see as the key development needs and strengths of the participant. However, the overall rating for each dimension is less crucial in a developmental centre than the individual ratings and comments. There need be less agonizing to agree an overall rating. As with the promotion centre, assessors should agree before the meeting who is going to write each participant's report. All of the rating sheets for a participant can be handed over to the report writer, who can write a considered report after the meeting.

A logical departure at a truly developmental centre is to have the participant present at the assessors' meeting, and to arrive at a joint report which is owned by the participant. The main difficulties will be the time required for each meeting and the assessors' embarrassment at feeling that they have to vet everything they might say about a participant. However, if the goal is development, these do not seem weighty objections.

If the assessment centre is for selection, research suggests that it is technically better to use a mathematical formula to combine scores on the individual dimensions for making decisions instead of having a discussion by assessors. The scores for the dimensions are put into a formula (which might be a simple or weighted average) to arrive at the decision. For example, Feltham (1988c) demonstrates the superiority of the mathematical composite score over assessors' decisions for predicting five performance criteria. One reason for the superiority of the mathematical method might be that the process of arriving at a group consensus involves the phenomenon of group dynamics. For example, Sackett and Ryan (1985) point out that the mechanical approach avoids any pulling of rank by a more powerful assessor over the others. An example of group dynamics at the assessors' meeting is provided by Herriott *et al* (1985). They got groups of four assessors to make a pre-discussion rating of participants; to have their discussion; and then to give a final rating individually. They found that the more powerful assessors are less likely to shift their ratings after the group discussion, and that an assessor who is an exception is more likely to shift downwards than upwards.

Despite the evidence, I prefer to have assessors make the decision. If the centre is for external selection, assessors can usually decide quite quickly by examining the profile, and it is more acceptable for them to do so than to arrive at a result by a formula. Building a computer algorithm to make the decision appears to be a state-of-the-art solution. However, it is a step that might well detract from the assessors' feeling that they have power in the decision. Certainly, there are problems of acceptability if the futures of internal people are decided by a computer, however superior that might be to assessors sitting in committee. From the assessors' point of view, the use of the computer ignores their need to feel they have done the right thing by each person and considered each case on its merits. A compromise is suggested by Goodge (1987) for the use of computers to produce averages and to highlight those individuals whom assessors need not spend time discussing. But is a computer really needed for this?

Assessors' reports

In development or promotion centres a report will usually be compiled out of the rating sheets. Normally, this report will be under the subheadings of the competency dimensions. However, in some cases the centre will be so developmental that a report is not required. The participant knows his or her developmental needs by the end of the centre and there is no need to record these formally. Indeed, the formal record might be seen as detracting from the achievement of the developmental goals of the centre.

Throughout the assessment centre the focus is on behaviour rather than on judgements. This is particularly important in the final write-up. To be useful for the participant the descriptions of strengths and development needs should maintain the focus on behaviour. When the assessor group has identified a strength or a development need, it is important to write about actual behaviour, giving as many examples as possible.

For example, the following description is behavioural and useful:

Strengths
Sensitivity: Throughout the group session and individual exercise she demonstrated a high level of sensitivity. For example, in the managers' meeting she was attentive to others and demonstrated that she listened to their needs and requirements. In the feedback exercise the subordinate felt he had a fair chance to say what he wanted. She showed empathy yet remained committed to increasing performance.

This description is useful because it focuses on actual behaviour, with examples across a range of exercises. On the other hand, the following description would not be helpful:

Weaknesses
Self-Confidence: A bad performance throughout, obviously a weakness. He is not confident with others and it shows!

The example is evaluative. He is described as 'bad' but it gives no example of what he actually did. Words like 'good' and 'bad' are judgemental rather than descriptive. They do not describe what happened but simply judge. Such comments will be difficult to feed back to participants and will fail to give them any clues about why they were good or bad or what they could do to modify their behaviour.

The report might also comment on the participant's overall performance in each exercise. If the exercises are designed around the different settings in which people work within the target job, it might well be that people perform better in some settings than others.

The usefulness of the assessment centre for development stands or falls by the quality of assessors' reports and of the feedback meeting. Unfortunately, there are all too many examples of centres that spend a lot of time and money on the centre itself, but then rush the report. I have seen assessors' reports that contain just a few clichés against each competency dimension, and read more like an end-of-term school report than something that can be useful for someone's development. The management development unit will receive copies of these reports and, if necessary, must institute special training in report writing.

Privacy

Discussion of the writing of assessors' reports introduces the issue of the appropriate control of their circulation and retention. As Finkle (1976) notes, 'when personal information is requested and disseminated with little or no evidence of need or of professional control, concerns for invasion of privacy may well arise' (p 883). He recommends basing a control policy on the clear 'identification of the principal type of decision to be made from the information' (p 883). For example, if the system is to identify long-term potential, there is no advantage in the current supervisor seeing the report. It will serve only to contaminate the appraisal process.

However, Finkle's advice should be tempered by the need to involve the supervisor in the process, so that he or she 'buys' into the development phase. As Rodger and Mabey (1987) observe, if line managers are alienated from the process they can be highly destructive. Ideally, line managers will be involved at the stage of development planning with their subordinate. They must not have been alienated so that at best they say development is nothing to do with them, or at worst they rule that there is no time for such activities.

An approach that could resolve this dilemma is to decide whose property the information is. If it is the participant's then he or she would be advised but not obliged to share it with the line manager. For truly developmental centres, the information might well be entirely the property of the participants. Indeed Herriot (1989) argues that even the information given by applicants to the organization should be seen essentially as their property. On the other hand, if it is the joint property of the participant and the management development function, both parties should agree to its being shared with others.

A second and related issue is how long the information remains on file. Rothwell (1985a) reports that BP removes reports after three years. However, for more enduring competency dimensions, the reports might be seen as having a longer validity, whereas for dimensions that should be developed after the centre, the validity will be only until the development has been undertaken.

11: Assessor Training

The whole assessment centre stands or falls by the quality of the assessors' work. The very best assessment centre exercise will be rendered useless by inadequately trained assessors. The key requirement at the centre is that they observe, record, classify and rate the behaviour of participants with accuracy. In addition, if the centre is for internal participants, assessors will probably give feedback to participants. They will need training in all these skills.

Assessor training timetable

I very much prefer assessor training to be residential. It avoids interruptions during the day and allows assessors to carry on their discussions into the evening. It is therefore probably cheaper than a non-residential course because it requires managers to give up fewer working days to be trained. It also helps build *esprit de corps* amongst the assessors.

Training in the assessment skills requires a full two days, and preferably three. Indeed, more time will be required if the training has to cover any complicated tests and inventories. To me it seems a false economy to jeopardize the assessment for the sake of a few hours of training.

The training in feedback and counselling will round the training up to a good week. An example of a timetable for assessor training that embodies these recommended times is contained in Figure 24.

In my view, these are the normal minimum times, which should only be reduced if it is a very brief centre, or if the assessors have had prior training. Certainly I cannot see how the training of four hours reported by Walsh *et al* (1987) for an assessment centre they studied could normally be adequate. By way of comparison, Cascio (1982) notes that training can last 'several weeks' (p. 245), and Russell (1985) quotes the example of a centre for which the training was three weeks. However, this might be going to the other extreme.

Figure 24
Example of timetable for assessor training

Day 1	
09.00–09.30	introduction to the course
09.30–12.00	the assessment centre approach the job analysis and competencies of the middle manager the assessment centre
12.00–13.00	introduction to observing, recording, classifying, and rating behaviour
14.00–15.30	video of subordinate 1:1 exercise: observe; record and classify
16.00–18.00	rating the subordinate 1:1 exercise
18.00–18.30	review of exercise
18.30–19.30	the in-tray exercise I
Evening	mark in-tray answers
Day 2	
09.00–12.00	the in-tray exercise II
12.00–13.00	the managers' meeting exercise I
14.00–16.30	the managers' meeting exercise II
17.00–19.30	the analytical exercise I
Evening	mark analytical exercise answers
Day 3	
09.00–11.00	the analytical exercise II
11.00–13.00	subordinate 1:1 exercise, video 2
14.00–16.30	group negotiation exercise
17.00–19.30	the assessors' meeting and recommendations
Evening	complete Myers-Briggs Type Indicator and FIRO-B
Day 4	
09.00–09.30	the Egan model of counselling
09.30–11.30	introduction to feedback and phase I counselling skills
11.30–13.00	score and debrief on Myers-Briggs Type Indicator and FIRO-B
14.00–19.30	counselling a problem area
Day 5	
09.00–10.00	phase II counselling skills
10.15–12.15	feedback of poor performance
12.30–13.00	phase III counselling skills
14.00–14.30	the career development system
14.30–16.30	career counselling
17.00–18.00	final issues
18.00	close

Dugan (1988) found no detrimental effect on assessors of having two weeks of training instead of three. She suggests that this might be due to a ceiling effect whereby further training yields no extra improvement in assessors' skills.

The first assessor training course will definitely take longer than subsequent courses, because there will be many issues that have to be resolved and clarified. In addition, having not seen the centre in action, it will be harder for the course leader to be definitive in replying to all the many questions that will be asked.

Training areas

In America, the training of assessors is included in the 'Standards and ethical considerations for assessment center operations' (Task Force on Assessment Center Standards, 1980) which recommend that assessors have a thorough understanding of the assessment dimensions as well as skill in the observation, integration and evaluation of behaviour. The timetable in Figure 24 includes these major areas of assessor training.

Going through the sections of the timetable, I would make the following comments on what should be covered.

Introduction
The assessment centre should be placed within the context of the organization's HR system, and the fundamental purpose of the centre, whether it is selection or development, should be discussed.

The job analysis
Assessors should be made familiar with how the job analysis was carried out, and then at least two hours should be devoted to the competency dimensions. It is vital that assessors become completely familiar with the competency dimensions; they are the kernel of the system. It might well also be appropriate to have training exercises that reinforce the dimensions in the assessors' minds. One such is a behavioural classification exercise. This consists of a set of behaviours, each of which must be classified under one of the competency dimensions as a positive or negative example of the dimension. A second exercise is a behaviour-generating exercise in which assessors produce examples of positive and negative behaviour for each competency. Apart from these exercises, the most important learning will come from discussing the competency dimensions and

the distinctions between them.

The assessment centre approach
Having gone through the competency dimensions required for the job or job level, the assessment centre approach should be introduced as the means of measuring the dimensions. It might be approached in a brief run-through of the main approaches to assessment, which can end on the cheering note that assessment centres combine a number of other approaches (eg interviews, tests, self-assessment), but lay heavy emphasis on getting people actually to perform in simulations of the target-level job. Assessment centres give the best of all worlds, and that is what gives them their unique power of prediction. Some of the evidence in favour of assessment centres can then be summarized, as well as what can go wrong, perhaps ending on the motivating thought that these pitfalls can be countered by good assessor training.

Skills of assessment
The main part of the assessor training is in the observation, recording, categorizing and rating of behaviour, which should be combined with the achievement of a good working knowledge of the exercises.

Observing and recording behaviour The key point to get across is that assessors need to have an accurate and complete record of what the participants did and said in the interactive exercises. (In the written exercises participants themselves provide the record.) Having this record means that assessors can back up their ratings with evidence at the assessors' meeting and at feedback meetings. Of course, they should not aim for a verbatim transcript, but they must have an adequate record. One approach to getting the message across to assessors is to ask them to imagine they had to justify their ratings to an enquiry.

Apart from being necessary for the meeting and for feedback, the process of recording helps the assessor concentrate on observing the participants. It also helps counter people's natural tendency to judge and rate participants rather than just observing them. This will help overcome the pitfalls to accurate observation and recording, such as:

- *The halo effect.* A favourable or unfavourable impression in one dimension (eg neatness of appearance) clouds one's judgement of the other dimensions.

- *The primacy effect.* Early observations count for more than later ones.

- *Stereotyping.* The participant's membership of a particular category leads to characteristics being imputed to him or her that are supposed to be typical of that category (eg the participant is a woman; women are sensitive; therefore the participant is probably good on sensitivity).

- *Implicit personality theory.* We carry around ideas of how dimensions go together, so that information on one dimension allows us to make inferences to other dimensions. Whilst the dimensions might go together more often than not, assessors must judge each dimension on its merits in case the person being assessed is one of the many exceptions to the rule.

This is all standard material for assessor and interviewer training. The points to emphasize are the dual needs to concentrate, and to leave rating/judgement/evaluation to the end. Taking good notes enable both these needs to be met. It will also deliver the raw material for feedback and for the assessors' meeting.

Assessors should practise observation and recording by looking at one of the videotapes. If the centre includes one-to-one exercises, it is better to use one of these than a video of a group exercise, because assessors will only have to concentrate on one person. It is best to start with about 15 minutes of the tape, which should be played through with assessors taking observation notes. The tape can then be rewound and played again to allow them to flesh out their notes. During this exercise, the trainer should check that assessors are taking adequate notes. An eye should be kept on the volume of notes everyone is taking, and the trainer should also make sure that the notes are not judgemental and evaluative. There should be no concession on the need for adequate non-judgemental notes! Once assessors have been through the tape in full, there needs to be a discussion of key learning points.

Classifying and rating After the observation and recording phase, assessors must classify their observations against the competency dimensions being measured in that exercise. They should concentrate on the dimensions that the exercise is targeting. However, particularly good evidence of any additional dimensions should also be classified.

I try to get assessors to move as quickly as possible to making margin notes of the competency classification whilst they are observing. It is far easier to classify at the time what was revealed by the observation than to leave it until later. However, right at the beginning of training they will have to postpone classifying until after they have completed their observing. Otherwise their decisions on classifying will interfere with the observation process.

The first time, about one hour will be needed to classify and to collate the evidence of the individual competencies on the rating sheet. The tape might be played once more to let assessors add to their observation notes, and to help them classify.

Once the classification is complete and any points discussed, assessors should make ratings from their evidence. It is crucial to impress on them the need for everyone to use the same rating scale so that like is being compared with like when the scores given by different assessors are compared. Assessors should rate their evidence, and the ratings by different assessors should be compared. It is better not to dwell on minor disagreements at this stage, but major discrepancies must be discussed. For example, if one person has the competency rated as a definite strength (a 4) and another has it as a definite weakness (a 2) these two assessors should compare their evidence. The person who gave 2 should outline the negative evidence and the person giving a 4 should outline the positive. Disagreements over ratings can often be tracked back to misclassifying evidence. In that case, assessors should be reminded of the indicators for the competency dimensions.

Hopefully, there will be an encouraging level of agreement in the ratings, and this will certainly hearten the assessors (as well as the trainer!).

I normally move on to one of the written exercises, and get the assessors to mark one of the answers done on the trial day. Marking will probably take at least 45 minutes the first time, after which assessors can compare their marks. Two hours should be allowed for the whole process for the first answer. After a break, they should mark another answer to the same exercise, with the aim of doing it faster.

The last type of exercise for them to practise is the group exercise. Assessors need to observe and rate the two people upon whom the video-recording concentrated. Again, ratings should be compared and differences discussed.

By this stage assessors will have covered the three different types of exercise, and should be developing some confidence in their abilities to assess people. They will be able to get further practice in the skills of assessment by going through and familiarizing themselves with any further written exercises included in the centre, together with other one-to-one and group exercises.

Interviews and tests

The training will also need to cover the interview, and to make assessors familiar with any tests or inventories that are being used. If the assessors are only giving feedback on the exercises, they do not need a detailed knowledge of the tests, but they certainly need to know enough to make use of the scores at the assessors' meeting. Indeed, if any complicated tests or inventories are used, several hours will be needed to make assessors familiar with them.

If the assessors are to give the feedback on the test and to help the participant integrate information from the test with exercise performance, some considerable time will be needed to train them, and it should only be attempted for a very simple test. Assessors cannot be turned into experts on psychological measures in a few hours or even a few days. If a complicated personality measure is included in the centre, it will be necessary for someone with expertise to interpret its meaning to the assessors' meeting, and for that person to carry out the feedback with the participant after the assessor has fed back the results of the behavioural exercises.

Assessors' meeting

The assessor training should also cover the assessors' meeting, including the collation of marks from the different exercises, and how the chairperson will lead the discussion through each candidate. The main point that the assessors' training is likely to raise is how decisions are taken after the marks for each competency dimension have been resolved.

Feedback and counselling

Apart from the training in the skills of assessment, assessors will also need training in the skills of feedback and counselling if they are to be their responsibility. The intention is not that they become expert counsellors. Rather, they must build upon the skills they need anyway if they are to be good assessors and managers. In particular, they must learn to listen and to empathize. They must also learn to give feedback that will be useful to the participant. As Boehm (1985) says, to be useful, feedback must be detailed, behaviourally specific, and related to job demands. It must concentrate on particular instances of good and bad performance in the competency dimension. It must also be given in a provisional and tentative way, rather than dogmatically, and it should concern areas about which the person can do something, rather than matters that are unalterable. In essence, the content of good feedback is the same as the content of a good report.

The training on feedback and counselling should be carried out over at least two days – and possibly longer – with plenty of practical work. It is important that assessors learn to give participants feedback with sensitivity. They must also be able to discuss the career implications of the assessment. Here the balance must be struck between what is proper for assessors to do, and what is the role of the management development manager. It might be appropriate for assessors to give feedback on the exercises and leave the management development professional to integrate this with any psychological and self-insight instruments that have been used, and to look at career path plans and options.

The training in feedback and counselling will need to include the nature of good feedback and what is an effective counselling relationship. It will also need to cover basic communication skills, particularly the skills of active listening. A useful model for counselling is that provided by Egan (1986), and the stages of counselling in his model should be covered. A simplified treatment of Egan's approach, with particular reference to counselling at work is provided by Reddy (1987).

The assessor and feedback training might be split rather than requiring assessors to be away from their jobs for a week. Aside from this convenience, splitting the training also allows assessors to consider any points arising from the first part of the training for discussion at the second part. However, there should not be a big gap between the two blocks of training. Assessors should use their skills of assessment as soon as possible after their training. Training should be scheduled so that at least some of the newly trained assessors are able to be at an assessment centre within a month, and the remainder as soon as possible after that.

12: After the Centre

The usual follow-up to the centre is the feedback of assessors' views, the drafting of a development plan, and its simple implementation.

Feedback on exercise performance

The need to give feedback to participants extends to all centres. Feedback might well be offered even to external people who have attended a selection centre, but who are not to be offered employment. In this case, the feedback need not be lengthy and certainly must not turn into a dispute or negotiation. Probably it is best handled centrally by the HR function. Such feedback is a courtesy, and one which might well bear a return by enhancing the organization's reputation amongst applicants. This will spread quickly amongst tight-knit groups such as graduates.

People who are selected and join the organization via an assessment centre should be given a fuller feedback on their performance once they have joined the organization. Obviously this should be a reasonably up-beat feedback and it will normally be carried out by someone from the HR function. It can include one or two areas that the new recruits should consider for development, and it can also be used as a way of discussing their initial posting (which might capitalize on their strengths).

In the case of promotion centres, the feedback should be given as soon as possible after the centre, preferably the next day and certainly within a week. The feedback on the exercises at internal centres is normally given by the assessors. They were the people who observed and rated the participants, and they should give the feedback. This makes for much more direct feedback of the assessment than if it was given by, say, the management development manager, who would have to report second hand on what the assessors saw. Having the assessors take responsibility also makes the assessment quite clearly a line function, rather than one belonging to management development.

Assessors might also make a start on discussing the career implications of the assessment centre with the participant. However, the major part of this will probably fall to the management development function.

The most important consideration with centres used for promotion is to retain the motivation of people who are, after all, amongst the organization's most able employees at their level. The danger lies in giving a lot of these people the impression that they have 'failed'. It is most important that the feedback is carried out in a way which avoids this outcome. The inherent tensions in promotion centres are the very reason that many organizations are using internal centres much more as an impetus to development than as the decisive event for promotion and the labelling of potential. However, it is pointless trying to fudge the issue if the performance at the centre is going to make a major contribution to promotion decisions in the near future. Everyone will know this anyway.

If the centre is truly developmental, the feedback might well be at the centre, perhaps after each exercise in a collaborative meeting between assessors and participants. In such cases, it makes sense to have no report and to keep everything that happens there confidential to participants. People will be free to try out different approaches to the exercises, agree a feedback there and then with assessors, and perhaps have another attempt at the exercise, trying out a new agreed approach. This will be a radical step for many organizations, but it is one that an increasing number are taking.

Career implications

The management development function can take over once the feedback on exercise performance has been carried out. It might well be appropriate to discuss the person's career ambitions and possibilities, as well as to go into detail on their development priorities. The aim is to achieve the mutual definition of expectations about the participants' careers. There will also need to be an integration of the person's exercise performance with his or her responses to any tests and inventories that were used at the centre. Finally, the person's self-assessments should be discussed in the light of the exercises and other measures. All this adds up to a quite complex feedback agenda, and counselling skills are particularly important so that participants are helped to see their options for themselves rather than being told them.

There is a danger in exaggerating the counselling that is involved. I am not suggesting that the organization turns into a deeply introspective collection of people undergoing analysis. However, some people going through a centre will find the feedback at odds with or a challenge to their expected career path. Indeed, as Gratton (1984) observes, 'There may be occasions when people need to be referred to a skilled professional counsellor.' (p 9) Even if the centre is basically developmental (ie there are no direct implications for promotion or potential), there will still be indirect implications. For example, some participants will be asking themselves, 'If that is what I am like, am I really going to get as far as I had assumed?' People are very good at hiding any feeling of hurt and upset. However, beneath the facade there will be people who are demoralized as a result of their attendance at the centre. If only from an economic point of view, that is an undesirable state of affairs. They will underperform, and might leave. Macho organizations might say good riddance, but few can afford the luxury of this response nowadays.

Development planning

Integrated with the feedback on performance and the consideration of career implications, should be the consideration of the development opportunities open to the participants. This is the message of hope, and for many centres it is their main focus. Assessors will need to be thoroughly familiar with the developmental options open to participants so that they can carry out initial discussions with the participant. For this to happen, of course, the developmental opportunities must be in place! The discussion with assessors will be followed up by the management development function. The overall goal must be that participants work out for themselves a plan over which they feel ownership and commitment. To do this, they must see for themselves the areas of development need, and work out ways of overcoming their needs which they see as useful and practicable. This ownership of development needs will only happen if all the earlier stages of the process, from the definition of the competencies through to the assessor feedback are working correctly. For example, people will not take on board a need to develop a competency that is plainly unnecessary to successful performance.

It is important that line managers are informed properly on the nature of the centre and the management development system. They will then be able to carry out their role, which is to agree with participants the development actions that the participant will be taking, and give these actions active support. If this is to happen, line managers must feel involved in the management development process. Otherwise, there is the danger of managers coming out with dreadful clichés like 'Now you're back in the real world' to participants.

Development actions

There is a series of integrated management development activities that should follow the centre. Indeed the follow-up to the centre is probably far more important than the centre itself. It is in the follow-up that the major developmental effort will take place. Unfortunately, with all too many centres, there is little systematic follow-up, with the result that many potential benefits of having the centre are lost. Furthermore the follow-up system must be installed before the centre. Otherwise participants are being asked to live on promises.

Aside from changes of job, and entry to special development schemes for a few people, one development system that can cope with the majority of participants will be a set of highly practical competency development workshops coupled with a system of action learning. The system is clearly focused on the competencies, and is designed to assist people to understand and acquire higher-performing behaviours for each competency. Clearly, it will not turn an extremely weak competency into a major strength, but it can certainly yield significant improvements.

Competency development should be an on-going activity. It needs to be a process of continuous development (Wood, 1988). Once participants have improved one competency, they will hopefully be keen to select another and decide the activities to develop it.

Behavioural workshops

It is possible to have separate workshops to concentrate on each particular competency and give the participants intensive coaching. Alternatively, some of the competencies might be grouped together and dealt with at a joint workshop. Different labels might be employed for the competencies and the workshops, but the relationship between them must be clear. For example, 'sensitivity' might be dealt with at the 'listening skills' workshop. Participants should attend the workshop early in their development programme and then the action learning allows them to practise the new competence that they acquire.

Each workshop should be behaviourally based. Both the workshops and action learning emphasize learning to be competent rather than learning about the competency. Learning about the competency is not the primary goal. It might well be a spin-off from the workshops, but it will come mainly from a possible third component of the development package, which is a competency-based reading list.

The workshops relate directly to the competencies of the organization. Having gone to all the trouble of finding the dimensions that mark out the high performer, it seems thoroughly worthwhile to invest in courses and workshops tailored to their development. The danger is that organizations with an existing system of development will be reluctant to start afresh with the competency list, but that might well be what is needed to ensure proper coverage of the competencies.

A suite of specially designed competency workshops has a number of advantages over trying to make do with existing courses, and over sending people away to take part in a generic course at an educational establishment. Each workshop need only take participants away from their work for two to four days, depending on the competency. The workshops are highly practical, and involve the acquisition or development of the specific behavioural skills that make up the competency for the organization. Participants will see that the workshop is a direct and specific answer to their competency development needs. Furthermore, the system emphasizes to participants that development is a continuing process. Once one competency has been addressed and developed they move on to the next one.

The workshops can be at different levels and can be integrated with a series of assessment centres. For example, an organization could have a set of workshops following an entry level centre to present the core skills of the competencies, and then have another set following a middle-level centre to build on the competency development. Apart from its overall coherence, this system means that people come to the middle centre having been able to make specific preparation on the competencies. This is a more logical order when the aim is for the organization to get an indication of potential from the middle centre. It is not measuring competency deficits that could have been remedied easily.

To summarize, the basic approach is to have one workshop for each competency, although some competencies might be combined. Ideally, there would be separate suites of workshops for the different levels of management. Certainly one level of provision would come after the junior or graduate assessment centre; another after the middle management centre. The workshops would be short and intensive, and would concentrate upon the acquisition or development of behavioural skills. They would be complemented by reading on the one hand, and action learning on the other.

Implementing the workshops
Because they are so strongly oriented to practical work, the implementation of these workshops need not be onerous. The most direct way of doing it is to have a project team for the overall project and a small design team for each workshop which would do the bulk of the detailed work. Finally, delivery teams – which would include the design team – would deliver the workshops.

Action learning
There are well-documented examples of action learning schemes, which are essentially project-based, and perhaps take participants away from their regular activities for months, (see, for example, Casey and Pearce, 1977, on action learning at GEC). The more elaborate schemes will necessarily be limited in the numbers that can benefit from them. It is therefore necessary to adapt the system for larger numbers. One possibility is for action learning to take the form of the participants doing an aspect of their existing jobs with a much greater consciousness of the competency they are trying to develop and exhibit. For example, if the job involves even minor project work, and they want to develop their competency at planning and organizing, then they might increase this competency by deliberately setting out to list the phases of each project, and work out the resources that are needed, and the timing etc. Alternatively, action learning might involve participants taking on a new activity at work that helps develop the targeted competency. For example, it might be that oral communication is the competency being focused on. A person working in a branch office might volunteer to make presentations to staff in the branch on communications from head office.

Participants must think carefully about the competencies they wish to develop, and how this can best be achieved in their particular place of work. The choice will need to be facilitated, probably at the end of the assessment centre. The action learning session would start by getting participants to break down their jobs into the component tasks. These tasks can be written as the left hand rows on a task × competency matrix. Along the top, and making up the columns will be the list of competencies. Participants then match competencies against the tasks, which will enable them to see how they can develop particular competencies within their own jobs. The matrix also allows participants to see at a glance which competencies they require most in their jobs, and this information will help them settle their development priorities. Participants can also consider taking on additional duties which involve tasks that are particularly relevant to developing the competencies. The methodology for choosing action learning can be repeated whenever the participant changes job.

Action learning is primarily up to the participants to organize and monitor. If the participants are not really keen to develop, action learning is likely to be ineffective. They should also be keen to find out how their development is progressing. To do this they should get the person most able to observe their behaviour in their action learning to rate them on the nominated competency, and give them feedback. For example, if they are developing presentation skills, they might get a colleague to observe their presentations and rate them, and discuss the rating. The system could be linked in with a process of mentoring (Clutterbuck, 1985), whereby the mentor guides and offers feedback to the learner.

Other development opportunities

The system of behavioural workshops and action learning is designed to cater for everyone going through the assessment centre process. It means that there is a system to address any weaknesses identified at the centre, and it is essentially a remedial system. Equally, of course, there should be a system for building on and capitalizing on people's strengths. This system might include sending high-potential people away to business schools and to shorter management courses, as well as ensuring that they have developmental job changes. Again, the focus should be on competency development, but for this system the competencies will be those required by the senior and general manager.

Feedback to the planning system

The ultimate aim of the centre itself and of the management development system is to ensure that the organization has the resources it needs when it needs them. This goal must not be lost sight of. The management development function will need to keep track of the person's performance at the centre and of their development following the centre. It is important that improvements in particular competencies after the centre are evaluated and recorded.

It is also important that people's own career aspirations are fed into the information system. There is no point in earmarking someone for the future role of general manager if he or she really wants to follow a more technical career path.

All the information should come together within a system of career path and succession planning. Indeed, even if the assessment centre is not used to make immediate decisions about individuals, I have suggested that it is crucial as a means of pencilling in people's likely career. Whilst some people will have more glorious careers than the centre predicted and others will do less well, the planning function will have a good idea of the overall resources available, and of significant gaps and gluts.

13: Validating the Centre

It is important that the centre is validated, which means simply that there needs to be a check that it is doing what it was intended to do. In deciding the way to validate the centre, it is therefore important to return to its original purpose. It might have been for selection, in which case the most appropriate validation is whether the centre is measuring the competency dimensions efficiently, and whether these measurements are related to future performance. A quite different validation will be required if the centre is intended to provide an impetus to the management development programme. If this is the aim, I would advance the controversial argument that it does not matter so much if the assessments are accurate as long as they provide a spur to individuals and to the organizational culture in the direction of development.

It can be seen already that there are a number of strands to the validation work that might be undertaken. Broadly these will fall under the headings of qualitative and quantitative validation. In addition, there is an audit against best practice, which determines whether the centre is at least set up in a way which is likely to work.

Qualitative validation

Qualitative research will concentrate on the reactions of participants and assessors to the assessment centre. The focus will be on how people experience the centre, and whether it is achieving its qualitative aims.

Validation with assessors

The questions for assessors will cover whether the centre was, for them, time-tabled correctly or stressful and rushed; whether the exercises seemed relevant and fair; how easy assessors found the exercises to mark; whether assessors felt the exercises were measuring the dimensions they were meant to; and whether assessors believe the centre is fulfilling its developmental purpose.

Validation with participants

Participants should be asked about their experience of the centre itself as well as about the helpfulness of the pre-centre briefing, and of the post-centre feedback and development planning. The questions will also cover the accommodation, travel etc. In short, the topics will readily suggest themselves, and these can be tackled by questionnaire or interview.

The time to start asking these questions is at the end of the centre, when there should be a debrief of participants. They can fill in – anonymously if they wish – a form to give their immediate reactions to the centre. They should also have a chance to discuss their views, perhaps over a drink. The debrief should be with the most neutral person at the centre, and usually that is the chairperson. However, if the centre is very developmental, it might be sensible for the assessors to be present so that the debrief is more collaborative.

It is also a good idea to have a longer-term feedback, perhaps after a month, when a follow-up questionnaire can be used to find out participants' considered feelings about the centre.

The feedback from participants should be taken seriously. Most of the complaints of participants are salutary and deserve consideration. If the centre is switching off applicants or staff, there is a clear problem. If a number of adverse reactions are received, the format of the centre should probably be altered. Alterations will usually entail changing the emphasis or presentation of the centre, rather than a radical rethink of the exercises. The price of leaving it unaltered will be people leaving the organization or being demotivated and performing poorly.

The questioning of participants is a critical part of the validation of selection centres. It helps determine whether the centre combines acceptability alongside any technical quantitative validity that it might enjoy. Indeed, qualitative validation will probably outweigh the quantitative evidence for a centre that has a developmental purpose. If the aim is to assess people on the target job dimensions so that they can agree areas for development need and get on with developing those areas, the crucial question is whether the centre helped the participants advance these aims.

Validation with the organization

The co-ordinator of the centre will also want to be aware of line managers' reactions to it, as well as the views of potential participants.

For example, people might be put off coming to an internal centre because they have heard that it can be stressful and threatening. The co-ordinator should know about the centre's image generally in the organization.

Quantitative validation

Quantitative research might of course be carried out on the qualitative data mentioned above, but the real technical validation deals with the analysis of the relationships among the assessment ratings, and between the assessment ratings and other quantified data. A number of statistics can be computed after the centres have run on, say, 60 people. These analyses should be rerun as the numbers build up, but the process should start early to give an early warning of any problems.

The individual ratings

First, the mean and standard deviation should be computed for each cell in the rating matrix, (eg on the ratings for sensitivity in the subordinate one-to-one exercise, and the ratings for sensitivity in the group exercise). Comparing the means for the same competency dimension measured in different exercises will show whether a particular dimension gains higher marks in one of the exercises in which it is marked than in another.

The standard deviations will show if assessors are differentiating between participants or giving everyone pretty well the same mark. It might be uniformly very low or very high, suggesting that the exercise is at the wrong level of difficulty for that competency dimension. On the other hand, if all the marks are around the middle of the range, this is usually a sign that assessors are not really able to measure the dimension in the exercise, and are seeking safety in the middle mark. Whatever the explanation, if there is little differentiation between people the measurement is in practice of no particular use. The way the competency dimension is brought out in the exercise will need to be changed, or assessors will need additional training. As a last resort the dimension might have to be measured in one of the other exercises.

Another way to find out whether raters are using the scale as intended, or being too severe or too lenient, or keeping their rating in the middle of the scale, is to examine the percentage of people being given each of the possible ratings for each cell in the ratings' matrix. For example, if the rating scale is as defined in Chapter 10, about

35–40 per cent of ratings would be expected to be 3; 20–25 per cent would be expected to be 2 or 4, and about 10 per cent would be expected to be 1 or 5. Anything markedly different would suggest that some further assessor training is in order if it cannot be explained by the ease or difficulty of the exercise, or a particularly good or weak group of participants. The statistics that are computed will have various possible explanations, and it will be a matter of judgement to decide which is the most plausible. For example, the mean for one competency dimension – say communication skill – might be 4, and only 1 per cent of ratings might be 1. This could be because of an excellent course in communication, so that participants are generally very good on this dimension. Alternatively, it might be very easy to do well in that dimension in the exercise. The calculation of the statistics will prompt these questions, but it cannot answer them.

Exercises and dimensions

The mean and standard deviation should be computed for the ratings for each exercise averaged across dimensions, and for each dimension, averaged or resolved across exercises. The means for the exercises will show whether some exercises are performed at a higher standard than others – perhaps because they are easier. The standard deviations will show the amount of differentiation between participants. Likewise, the dimension means will show whether some dimensions gain higher ratings than others, and the standard deviations will show the amount of discrimination between participants for each competency dimension.

Once enough people have been through the centre, all these statistics can be computed separately for participants with different backgrounds in the organization. For example, it might be found that people from the marketing function do better on the customer exercise than people from personnel. The data will show what is happening and then it is a matter of deciding whether it is reasonable or whether some amendments need to be made to the exercises.

The exercise effect

If the grid of ratings is factor analysed, the hope would be to find one factor for each of the assessment dimensions. The expectation is that the ratings for each dimension across exercises would all be correlated. However, what is found quite typically is separate factors for each exercise. The ratings across competency dimensions that are measured in a particular exercise 'go together' and form a factor. This phenomenon will be considered in more detail in Chapter 14. For the moment, the first thing to ask is whether assessors' discrimination between dimensions within each exercise can be increased by further assessor training. Alternatively, the exercise effect might be due to a problem with the exercises. For example if a group exercise is trying to measure various cognitive competencies, then the person who says little or nothing might well be marked down against a broad sweep of competency dimensions, thus creating the exercise effect. A further approach to the exercise effect would be to check that the competency dimensions are worded clearly, and that they are clearly separated from each other in their definitions.

Dimension scores and their components

The correlation between the assessors' resolved ratings for a dimension across exercises and the simple sum of the ratings across exercises will show the extent to which all the discussion that goes into resolving a score for the dimension could be dispensed with, simply by adding the scores up. It also shows the extent to which assessors are moving away from the individual scores in arriving at their resolved scores. A model of the process leading to the assessors' resolved rating can be derived by regressing the individual ratings for the competency in the different exercises onto the assessors' resolved rating. This will show whether particular exercises contribute more than others to the assessors' resolved rating for the competency dimension.

In addition, the scores in each of the competency dimensions can be correlated with the overall assessment centre rating. One or two competency dimensions might be found to exhibit very low correlations with the total, which would suggest that these dimensions contribute little in the minds of the assessors in forming their overall rating. The results of these analyses should be discussed with assessors, and there should be a decision on whether the devaluing of some dimensions is desirable. If not, drawing the issue to the attention of assessors should contribute to its correction.

Redundancy of dimensions

A very high correlation between the overall ratings for two dimensions suggests either that they are in fact so closely related that one of them is redundant, or that they are not being differentiated in the minds of the assessors. If the distinction is meaningful and important there will be a need for additional assessor training.

Assessment ratings and tests and inventories
The assessment ratings should be examined in relation to scores on the cognitive tests and personality inventories that are being used. The tests and inventories will have been chosen because of their assumed relationship to the competencies, and these assumptions should now be checked. If no relationship is found between the test's scores and the competencies, the value of the test to the assessors' decision appears very doubtful.

Criterion validation
Many people would regard the relationship between the assessment ratings and subsequent performance as the most telling part of the validation exercise. The assessment should yield valid indications of the competency dimensions, and performance on these should lie behind overall job performance. The exercise effect casts doubt on whether the link to performance is as straightforward as this, but the pragmatic question might be 'Does it work?', rather than 'Why does it work?'

The speediest answer will be obtained by examining the correlations between the competency dimensions as measured by the assessors at the centre and as measured by the participants themselves, and by their line managers. The difficulty in drawing conclusions from these statistics, however, is that it is unknown which set of ratings is most accurate. Indeed some of the dimensions might only be clearly visible after the person has moved into the job or job level on which the centre was targeted.

It is therefore more logical to wait and correlate assessment centre scores with future performance. However, it will often not be possible to reach firm conclusions even from these correlations, because of the practical constraints on having a neat design for assessment centre research. One problem is what might have happened between the assessment centre and the people's assumption of the target-level jobs. For example, they will have attended development workshops etc. Furthermore, people who performed badly at the centre will not be included in the sample as they will not get through to the target level. Conversely, the people who performed well will go to the next level job and their performance will be known to others. This is the self-fulfilling prophecy effect, whereby people who perform highly become known as the rising stars. They get more developmental experience and go to the target job with people expecting and looking for the good news and excusing the bad.

In short, carrying out a validation study that will pass academic scrutiny is difficult. However, that should not mean abandoning the effort. At least the validation will prompt the right questions.

Developmental validation

If the centre is primarily for development, the key validation questions are whether any development takes place at the centre, and whether attending the centre acts as an impetus for subsequent development. In turn, these subsequent development activities should also be validated. The validation must determine whether people who attend the development modules or take part in action learning really improve their performance as shown for example through the performance appraisal system or perhaps at a subsequent assessment centre.

Validating existing centres

A centre that has been operating for some time should be examined to make sure that it is working properly. At the very least, there should be an analysis of the ratings that have been produced at the centre. Blackham and Smith (1989) provide a very good example of how such an analysis can lead to subsequent modifications of a centre. As Blinkhorn (1986) observes, the problems brought to light when the enlightened company audits its practices are likely to compare favourably with the problems of companies who prefer to remain in ignorance.

It might be found that assessors are not differentiating between people sufficiently on some dimensions for some exercises; an example is the centre mentioned in Chapter 5, which included self-monitoring as a dimension. None of the assessors really understood what was meant by this dimension, let alone how to rate it. Typically people got a rating of 3 on it. Problems like this will show up when the statistics are computed on the assessors' ratings.

An exercise effect might well be found when the ratings are factor analysed. For example, Blinkhorn (1986) cites an analysis of one company's centre for which the ratings on 12 dimensions revealed just one factor used by assessors in making decisions. Likewise, Blackham and Smith (1989) found that ratings on 10 dimensions yielded three consistent factors.

Inferential evidence: conformity to best practice

The validation work that has been suggested gives direct evidence of whether a centre is working. A different approach is to examine the centre to determine whether it is being operated correctly and in a way that should make it work properly. It is examined or audited against best practice.

A first aspect of best practice is the features of the centre that will or will not make it a reliable measure of people on the dimensions. In order to have validity, it is necessary that the assessment centre is reliable. This means that participants should make similar responses between one day and the next, and assessors should assess these responses the same way.

Making the same responses will depend on being presented with the same stimuli. Problems of reliability will come if, for example, role players differ amongst themselves in the part they are playing, or if the same role player chooses to play the part differently from day to day. Difficulties can also come if the exercises are constructed so that much of a participant's behaviour in the target competency dimensions depends on what the other participants are like. For example, a leaderless group discussion exercise might be used to measure 'leadership'. However, the amount of leadership manifested by any one participant will depend on the leadership of the other participants. The participant with average leadership might appear quite strong in an otherwise weak group, or weak in an otherwise strong group.

Steps to overcome these problems will include giving careful and comprehensive briefing and training to role players; not trying to measure competency dimensions in group exercises that clearly depend on the particular mix of people in the group; and setting up the group exercise in a way that minimizes the group mix effect, for example by including the light-touch chairperson.

Even if participants are presented with the same stimuli and respond in the same way from day to day, it is also necessary for these responses to be assessed in the same way by different assessors. If there is a lot of variation between assessors, the assessment will say more about the assessor than about the participant. The reliability of assessments is achieved by good assessor training, and by making exercises assessor-friendly. For example, I have discussed targeting items in an in-tray on specific dimensions so that assessors are in no doubt as to the dimension being marked.

Aside from reliability, validity will also depend on getting the competency dimensions right, and ensuring the fidelity of the exercises as a simulation of the target job. In the best-practice audit, there will be a need to review the competency dimensions to check that they are the critical dimensions for high performance in the job. There will also be a need to check the exercises. They should, as far as possible, correspond to the target job. There is, for example, no point in having quasi-military outdoor exercises as part of an accountants' assessment centre. Similarly, I was told of an assessment centre conducted in English for people whose mother-tongue was not English. Although it was argued that a good knowledge of English was important for the people being assessed, there was really no logic in letting a language problem prejudice the assessment of people's other competencies.

It is also important to ensure that assessors are focusing on the competency dimensions as they are defined and not their own images of suitability. Assessment centre decisions or recommendations must be based on performance on the competency dimensions. They must not be diluted by some sort of overview of the person against the image of a 'good type'. The overview will be likely to ignore performance on the expensively designed exercises.

All these aspects of best practice deal with the centre's usefulness as a means of assessment. Equally, there is the best practice for the developmental aspects of centres. This will focus largely on the way participants are treated; indeed whether they are called participants or candidates in the first place. It will also cover assessors' reports and feedbacks. The audit should examine a sample of reports to determine whether they are useful and developmental or a set of unhelpful generalities.

14: Current Issues and Developments

Assessment centres are very much a 'live' topic in the journals, particularly the *Journal of Applied Psychology*, *Personnel Psychology* and the *Journal of Occupational Psychology*. There are a number of issues and developments in these journals which have influenced the earlier chapters of this book, but which now merit discussion in their own right. I have deliberately introduced some of the terminology from the journals, but I have 'translated' it to make it more understandable.

The exercise effect

A problem for assessment centres noted in Chapter 13 is the exercise effect. The effect is found when ratings of assessment centres are analysed. Assessment centres are designed with the explicit expectation that there will be more agreement about the same dimension across exercises (called monotrait-heteromethod correlations) than about different dimensions within the same exercise (heterotrait-monomethod correlations). However, with the exercise effect, the analysis shows the opposite: there is more in common between ratings of different dimensions within each exercise than there is between ratings of the same dimension across exercises. Assessors seem to be paying more attention to an overall halo for each exercise than to making distinctions between dimensions. The most famous study showing the effect was by Sackett and Dreher (1982). They took the ratings of three different assessment centres and found, for each centre, that the heterotrait-monomethod correlations were larger than the monotrait-heteromethod correlations. The centres lacked convergent validity (viewings of the same dimension in different exercises did not converge on the same answer) and divergent validity (viewings of different dimensions within an exercise did not diverge from each other). When they factor analysed the matrix of correlations between individual ratings, they obtained exercise factors for all three centres.

In a related study, Turnage and Muchinsky (1982) examined a centre that rated all dimensions in all exercises. They found that the correlations between different traits within an exercise were about the same as the correlations between the same trait across exercises. Finally, Bycio *et al* (1987) examined a centre which had five exercises, and again found that exercises were dominant even after they had combined early overlapping dimensions. The conclusion (replicated by Robertson *et al*, 1987 in the UK) suggests that there is a pervasive halo across ratings within an exercise.

Indeed the pervasiveness of the effect was demonstrated by Silverman *et al* (1986) who appeared to do everything possible to destroy it. They got assessors to rate the candidates on the dimensions for each individual exercise only after the rating for each dimension across the exercises had been agreed. Even with this approach to rating, which is a modification of that used by AT&T, the correlations between exercises for individual dimensions were not much greater than the correlations between dimensions within exercises. Furthermore, when they factor analysed the matrix of correlations, they still did not obtain factors clearly corresponding to the dimensions.

There are various ways to react to the exercise effect. One is to try to improve the assessment process to get rid of it. A first step is to ensure that the dimensions can be revealed independently in each exercise. A lack of independence will be found, for example, in a group exercise in which one dimension (say lack of self-confidence) clouds the other dimensions that are being measured. The exercise effect will also be found if a dimension is not properly understood or if the dimensions are badly defined. Assessors will tend to use the other dimensions as a rough guide to a poorly understood one. If the dimensions are not separated from each other clearly in terms of their definitions, then it is most unlikely that there will be a differentiation between them in terms of ratings.

The effect could also be attributed to participants differing in their familiarity with the different exercise settings. For example, if a person is familiar with the one-to-one setting, performance might be better across a series of dimensions than for an exercise in which the setting is less familiar. This might be tackled by giving everyone the chance to practise and develop before the centre. For example, if one of the exercises is a subordinate meeting people without experience of this type of interview could be given some practice before the centre.

So the exercise effect should be met in the first instance by refinements to the processes of defining dimensions, revealing the dimensions via the exercises, and marking performance in the exercises. These refinements were not all present in the studies showing the exercise effect. First, it is possible that there was not the opportunity for participants properly to demonstrate all the dimensions in the exercises in which they were examined. This is particularly relevant to the studies by Turnage and Muchinsky, and Bycio *et al*, in which all dimensions were rated in all exercises. Secondly, it is possible that the assessor training was inadequate. For example Turnage and Muchinsky's assessors were trained for only two days.

The exercise effect leads some people to advocate rating by exercise rather than continuing to try to achieve valid ratings for each dimension. For example Herriott (1986) concludes that the rationale of rating by dimension is unsound, and that it is much better to ensure that the exercises give a valid sample of the job and to rate overall performance in each exercise. The centre becomes a series of work samples (Klimoski and Brickner, 1987), and task analysis is important as part of the job analysis (Robertson *et al*, 1987).

However, assessors' impressions of performance in an exercise must surely be mediated by dimensions. They do not simply say that someone did well in the in-tray. They say that the person did well in the in-tray because he or she communicated clearly, planned and organized etc. It therefore seems premature to give up on dimensions. Furthermore, feedback has to be in terms of the dimensions. Giving up is not an option if the centre is to be used for development (Bycio *et al*, 1987). For example, telling someone they need to improve in meetings with subordinates begs the question of what is wrong at the moment. The explanation must return to the dimensions of competence. The person needs to be told that it is listening skills or presenting a point of view that needs to be improved.

Reliability and validity

The basic findings on the validity of assessment centres was covered in Chapter 3. It was noted that the evidence tends to be summarized as showing the power of assessment centres. In fact, the position is more complex than that summary suggests, and relates back to the exercise effect. The evidence must be examined against the different types of validity that a centre might have.

Content and construct validity

The content validity of the centre is established if it can be shown to be a good and accurate simulation of the target-level job. Construct validity deals with the centre as a measure of the job dimensions presumed to underlie job performance. To build in both types of validity, Byham (1980) says that the centre must be based on a thorough job analysis to ensure that the exercises represent at the correct level of complexity the most common and significant job activities, and that the centre measures competency dimensions that are related to performance in important job activities. Furthermore, the dimensions must be observable in the exercises. Sackett (1987) adds the importance of proper training of assessors, and of putting all candidates on an equal footing by good instructions and briefing.

Developing an assessment centre along the lines laid out in this book does everything possible to promote construct and content validity. By way of contrast, construct validity is not assisted if generic dimensions are used without a proper check of their applicability to the target job, and content validity is not promoted if the centre consists of the Lego or piranha-ditch exercises, which bear little relationship to the job of a manager.

The problem is that although the textbook approach should give construct validity, the evidence from the exercise effect suggests that the effort is in vain. This leads Klimoski and Brickner (1987) to say, 'The available research consistently demonstrates a lack of evidence for the construct validity of assessment center dimension ratings.' (p 246)

Criterion validity

Assessment centres might not work by measuring the dimensions as planned, but they do seem to achieve their ultimate goal, which is to predict immediate performance in the job, or immediate ratings of potential, or performance over time (indexed by final level or final salary in the organization). Thus, they have a validity when judged against concurrent (concurrent validity) or future (predictive validity) criteria of performance.

An immediate problem with criterion validity was summed up by Robertson and Makin (1986) who said that 'for different reasons almost all of the current criteria with which we work are unsatisfactory' (p 52). Performance measures generally concentrate on the individual's own performance, and often this has to be rated by supervisors. Relying on ratings as the criterion measure means that negative evidence can always be explained away as due to a problem with the supervisors' ratings rather than with the centre.

One alternative criterion to performance is salary progression and promotion, which Meyer (1987) calls performance-over-time measures. In their favour, promotion decisions are frequently based on a collective judgement rather than on one supervisor's viewpoint. They are also cut and dried, carrying with them no errors of measurement. However, promotions and salary progress might not be linked closely to performance, and in some organizations are more a result of long service than ability. Indeed, Turnage and Muchinsky (1984) found only a weak relationship between performance and promotion.

The third commonly used criterion is ratings of potential. Studies of validity have tended to show a higher correlation between assessment centres and ratings of potential than between assessment centres and current performance. For example, Turnage and Muchinsky (1984) found potential ratings to be the criterion measures most highly correlated with assessment evaluations. Similarly Gaugler *et al* (1987) found higher validities for potential than for performance in their meta-analysis.

Explanations of criterion validity

The paradox is that assessment centres appear to predict criteria, but the exercise effect suggests that they do not do so by measuring the dimensions. This has led people to speculate on how they *do* work. One possibility is that assessors arrive at some kind of rating of overall performance in each exercise, and that these ratings relate to job performance because the exercises simulate the job. This is the obvious conclusion from the exercise effect, and in many ways is the most optimistic answer to how the centres work. At least it says that it is performance on the exercises which is the predictive variable. Other explanations are more gloomy. They suggest that the relationship between assessment centre marks and the criteria are based on an artifact.

One such explanation is advanced by Klimoski and Strickland (1977) and Gaugler *et al* (1987), who suggest that assessors and the people providing the criterion information hold in common a prototype of a good manager that intrudes on both the assessment centre ratings and ratings of potential and performance. Of course there would be no problem if the prototype was in terms of the assessment centre dimensions. The concern however is that it is a much grosser stereotype of a 'good type'. For example, Dobson and Williams (1989) are clear in their own minds that the British Army's assessment centre correlates with performance because the board concentrates on an overall rating of character, which will also be a major influence on ratings of subsequent performance. Any centre that follows the AT&T model of rating dimensions globally across exercises rather than taking one exercise at a time seems particularly susceptible to the intrusion of the 'good type' halo.

There is a more obvious explanation for the correlations between assessment centres and promotion than the 'good type' artifact, namely that the assessment centre performance is well known and leads on to the self-fulfilling prophecy of people labelled as good going on to raise their performance in line with the label, being given extra opportunities to develop, and benefiting from people perceiving them in terms of their label. The assessment centre result therefore leads to performance and to promotion, and is certainly not independent of the criteria it is meant to predict. Apparently contradicting this crude artifactual explanation are studies, notably the AT&T studies, which have kept the assessment centre results secret but which still found a relationship with promotion.

A further artifactual explanation is that assessors might be evaluating what they know of the individuals already, and using this as the basis for their assessment centre judgement. As Klimoski and Brickner (1987) point out, assessors have a good deal of information, from application forms in the case of external applicants, or from organizational repute in the case of internals. Past success might reasonably be expected to relate to future success.

Klimoski and Brickner (1987) also discuss the possibility that both assessment centre and job performance is determined by intelligence. This is not just the narrow psychologists' definition of intelligence but the broader concept of practical intelligence (Sternberg and Wagner, 1986; Wagner, 1987). This argument amounts to stating that the dimensions measured by the assessment centre are neither the dimensions that matter in the job nor those that matter at the centre. What matters in both cases is practical intelligence.

There is no neat answer to the debate about why assessment centres work. Indeed, Turnage and Muchinsky (1984) suggest that firm conclusions might be impossible with assessment centre research. One answer might be that different centres work for different reasons. In some cases, undoubtedly, both the centre and the performance criterion are saturated with whether or not the participant is a 'good type'. Other centres might just work by measuring the dimensions that underlie performance in the job. Certainly, I believe that this should still be the goal of assessment centre designers, who should do everything possible to achieve it. Assessors should be well trained, the dimensions must be clearly specified and kept simple, and the exercises must be well designed. The design of the exercises should enable the dimensions to be seen with confidence by assessors. In addition, the exercises should be good simulations of the job so that at least content validity will be achieved. In all, I feel far from pessimistic. However, it is clearly vital to question whether a particular centre is working only by an artifact such as measuring the organization's stereotype of a 'good type'.

Choosing the appropriate type of validity
It has been seen that assessment centres can be designed to achieve content validity by ensuring that they simulate the job. Furthermore, they are likely to have predictive validity, even if its basis is open to debate. However, Sackett (1987) points out that these different types of validity are not interchangeable. It is not enough just to establish any sort of validity and heave a sigh of relief. He says that content validity is particularly appropriate if the centre is being used to establish people's current level of competence to perform in the target-level job now or in the immediate future. Under these circumstances, the assessment centre is being used to sample the participants' competence. On the other hand, if the centre is being used to establish potential to perform at the target level in some years' time, Sackett says that criterion validity is more appropriate. There is no point in loading the centre with simulated activities that will be learned between the time of attending the centre and arrival in the target-level job. The centre should still simulate the job, but the learned components should be stripped out of the simulation, and a proper predictive validation is required to ensure that the centre is achieving its purpose.

Equal opportunities

The fidelity of exercises has importance under the American 'Uniform guidelines on employee selection procedures' (Equal Employment Opportunity Coordinating Council, 1978). These might serve as a guide to good practice in the UK even if the law is less stringent. All that the guidelines ask is that the assessment centre appears likely to work to select the best people for the job. That must be in everyone's interest. The approach to designing and validating assessment centres that has been described in this book falls within the guidelines. The centre is based on a careful analysis of the dimensions required for the job, and the exercises are based on job simulations. However, a centre might be held to be discriminatory if there were not a job analysis preceding it or if the exercises did not simulate the target job.

The actual evidence on the equality of impact of centres tends to be favourable (Huck and Bray, 1976; Ritchie and Moses, 1983). However, Walsh *et al* (1987) found that in the assessment centre they studied, females were rated more highly than males by male assessors. Various explanations might be advanced, but at least the study did not uncover an 'old boy' network.

An aspect of equality was investigated by Robertson and Iles (1988). Their hypothesis, based on an assumption of inequality, was that ratings of femininity in women would be negatively correlated with perceived appropriateness for 'male' jobs (including managerial jobs) whilst masculinity in men would be positively correlated with the same criterion. The hypothesis was investigated using 78 participants in a UK clearing bank's promotion centre, and was not upheld.

Current developments

Finally, what developments are taking place in assessment centres? The most obvious current development is the change of emphasis to assessment centres being something 'done with' participants rather than 'done to' them. Centres are becoming much more developmental and less threatening events. The new emphasis is on participants and assessors collaborating to identify the participants' strengths, development needs and areas which both see as weaknesses to be complemented by others in the team.

Of course, some centres will still be installed to choose internal people for promotion or to identify people with high potential. Those goals must recognize that there are bound to be mixed feelings about a centre which contributes very directly to promotion or to joining a fast stream. In future, these centres are likely to be as developmental as possible, trying to make sure that everyone comes away with some benefit even if it was only a greater self-understanding and a development plan.

In general, centres seem more likely to be used for 'pencilling in' people's likely career progression, rather than for making hard decisions. The more tentative nature of the assessment is reinforced by the changeability of the template against which the participants are assessed. It makes less and less sense to give people a seal of approval for the rest of their careers. The desired qualities will change as the role of a manager changes. The competency list should be continually questioned and updated, and people should attend assessment centres as a matter of routine to update their profiles, and decide their next career moves and development plans.

In the near future, generic lists of management competencies seem certain to emerge, as well as agreed lists for specific occupational groups (eg salespeople or supervisors). In turn this will make generic exercises more feasible, and these could be followed up by generic development workshops. However, these generic products will have to be customized to each organization so that they are owned and to ensure that they work within that particular organization.

There is also likely to be a greater use of computers and expert systems in conjunction with assessment centres. For example, *Personnel Management* (August 1989, p 14) carried a report of how British Nuclear Fuels managers had gone through an assessment process that examined 50 skills, characteristics and aspects of behaviour. The managers went through workshops with 15–17 events. The marks were fed into the computer which pointed out where differences between assessors lay. These were discussed and reconciled and the computer then averaged scores over events for the 50 skills. The pattern of strengths and weaknesses was considered against the profiles required for 23 different managerial jobs.

This is very seductive, if only because it is under control of the computer. Of course, some might ask whether the differences between jobs and between people were sufficient for the allocation process really to be statistically sensible. It is also important to be sure that there really were 50 dimensions and a need for 15–17 assessment events. Nevertheless, the availability of computers and expert systems seems to make this type of development inevitable.

It also seems likely that information technology hardware will become a normal part of the centre itself. For example, parts of in-trays could be presented interactively via a computer, faxes could arrive, or a screen could be up-dating the news. However, none of these possibilities should cause the principles of good exercise design to be lost sight of.

Aside from these developments at the practical level, it seems likely that academic research on assessment centres will continue to explore why they work, and hopefully there will be some progress on the conditions which help and hinder their working. In addition, future research could follow Robertson's (1985) plea for an examination of the different validities of the separate components of assessment centres. Although answers are beginning to appear (eg Brannick *et al*, 1989) we still do not know enough about the conditions under which, say, in-trays are more predictive than one-to-one exercises.

Bibliography

ADAMS, Dawn. (1987) 'Assessment centre exercises – bespoke or ready to wear?'. *Guidance and Assessment Review.* Vol 3, No 1, February 1987. pp 6–7.

ALEXANDER, Ralph A *and* BARRICK, Murray R. (1987). 'Estimating the standard error of projected dollar gains in utility analysis'. *Journal of Applied Psychology.* Vol 72, No 3, 1987. pp 475–9.

ANSTEY, Edgar. (1989) 'Reminiscences of a wartime army psychologist'. *The Psychologist.* November 1989. pp 475–8.

AUSTIN, Roger. (1986) 'Why assessment centres are often necessary'. *Guidance and Assessment Review.* Vol 2, No 1, February 1986. pp 5–7.

BEDFORD, Tol. (1987) 'New developments in assessment centre design'. *Guidance and Assessment Review.* Vol 3, No 3, June 1987. pp 2–3

BLACKHAM, R B, *and* SMITH, D. (1989) 'Decision-making in a management assessment centre'. *Journal of Operational Research Society.* Vol 40, No 11, 1989. pp 953–60.

BLINKHORN, Steve. (1986). 'Assessing management potential – retrospect and prospect'. *Guidance and Assessment Review.* Vol 2, No 6, December 1986. pp 1–3.

BOEHM, Virginia R. (1985). 'Using assessment centres for management development – five applications'. *Journal of Management Development.* Vol 4, No 4, 1985. pp 40–53.

BOUDREAU, John W. (1983). 'Effects of employee flows on utility analysis of human resource productivity programs'. *Journal of Applied Psychology.* Vol 68, No 3, 1983. pp 396–406.

BOUDREAU, John W. (1983) 'Economic considerations in estimating the utility of human resource productivity improvement programs'. *Personnel Psychology.* Vol 36, 1983. pp 551–76.

BOYATZIS, R. (1982) *The competent manager.* New York, Wiley, 1982.

BRANNICK, Michael T *et al.* (1989). 'Construct validity of in-basket scores'. *Journal of Applied Psychology.* Vol 74, No 6, December 1989. pp 957–63.

BRAY, D W. (1964). 'The assessment center method of appraising management potential' *in* BLOOD, D W *ed. The personnel job in a changing world.* New York, American Management Association, 1964.

BRAY, Douglas W. (1985). 'Fifty years of assessment centres: a retrospective and prospective view'. *Journal of Management Development.* Vol 4, No 4, 1985. pp 4–11.

BROGDEN, H E (1949) 'When tasting pays off'. *Personnel Psychology.* Vol 2, 1949. pp 171–83.

BYCIO, Peter *et al.* (1987) 'Situational specificity in assessment center ratings: a confirmatory factor analysis'. *Journal of Applied Psychology.* Vol 72, No 3, 1987. pp 463–74.

BYHAM, W C. (1980). 'Starting an assessment center the right way'. *Personnel Administrator.* February 1980. pp 27–32.

CASCIO, Wayne F. (1982). *Applied psychology in personnel management.* 2nd ed. Reston, Virg, Reston Publications, 1982.

CASEY, David *and* PEARCE, David. (1977) *More than management development: action learning at GEC.* Farnborough, Gower Press, 1977

CLUTTERBUCK, David. (1985) *Everyone needs a mentor: how to foster talent within the organization.* London, Institute of Personnel Management, 1985

COCKERILL, Tony. (1989) 'The kind of competence for rapid change'. *Personnel Management.* Vol 21, No 9, September 1989. pp 52–6

CRABB, Stephen. (1989) 'Man of the moment: David Duffield'. *Personnel Management.* Vol 21, No 12, December 1989. pp 36–7

CRONBACH, L J *and* GLESSER G C. (1965) *Psychological tests and personnel decisions.* 2nd ed. Urbana, Ill, University of Illinois Press, 1965

CRONSHAW, Steven F *and* ALEXANDER, Ralph A. (1985) 'One answer to the demand for accountability: selection utility as an investment decision'. *Organizational Behavior and Human Decision Processes.* Vol 35, 1985. pp 102–18

CURNOW, Barry. (1989) 'Recruit, retrain, retain: personnel management and the three Rs'. *Personnel Management.* Vol 21, No 11, November 1989. pp 40–7

DE SIMONE, Randy L *et al.* (1986) 'Accuracy and reliability of SDy estimates in utility analysis'. *Journal of Occupational Psychology.* Vol 59, 1986. pp 93–102

DOBSON, Paul *and* WILLIAMS, Allan. (1989) 'The validation of the selection of male British Army officers'. *Journal of Occupational Psychology.* Vol 62, Part 4, December 1989. pp 313–25

DUGAN, Beverly. (1988) 'Effects of assessor training on information use'. *Journal of Applied Psychology.* Vol 73, No 4, November 1988. pp 743–8

DULEWICZ, Victor. (1989) 'Assessment centres as the route to competence'. *Personnel Management.* Voil 21, No 11, November 1989. pp 56–9

DUNNETTE, Marvin D. (1966) *Personnel selection and placement.* Belmont, Calif, Wadsworth Publishing Co, 1966

EGAN, Gerard. (1986) *The skilled helper: A systematic approach to effective helping.* 3rd ed. Monterey, Brooks/Cole, 1986

EMERY, F E *and* TRIST E L. (1965) 'The causal texture of organizational environments'. *Human Relations.* Vol 18, 1965. pp 21–32

EQUAL EMPLOYMENT OPPORTUNITY COORDINATING COUNCIL. (1978) 'Uniform guidelines on employee selection procedures'. *Federal Register.* 1978. pp 38290–315

FELTHAM, Rob. (1988a) 'Validity of a police assessment centre: A 1–19-year follow-up'. *Journal of Occupational Psychology.* Vol 61, Part 2, June 1988. pp 129–44

FELTHAM, Rob. (1988b) 'Justifying investment'. *Personnel Management.* Vol 20, No 8, August 1988. pp 17–18

FELTHAM, Rob. (1988c) 'Assessment centre decision making: judgemental vs. mechanical'. *Journal of Occupational Psychology.* Vol 61, Part 3, September 1988. pp 237–41

FINKLE, Robert B. (1976) 'Managerial assessment centers' *in* DUNNETTE Marvin D *ed. Handbook of industrial and organizational psychology.* Chicago, Ill, Rand-McNally, 1976. pp 861–88

FLETCHER, Clive. (1989) 'The impact of demographic changes on selection'. *The Occupational Psychologist.* Vol 8, August 1989. pp 3–4

FONDA, Nickie. (1989) 'Management development: the missing link to sustained business performance'. *Personnel Management.* Vol 21, No 12, December 1989. pp 50–3

FOX, Shaul *et al.* (1989) 'Perceived similarity and accuracy of peer ratings'. *Journal of Applied Psychology.* Vol 74, No 5, October 1989. pp 781–6

FREDERIKSEN, Norman. (1986) 'Toward a broader conception of human intelligence'. *American Psychologist.* Vol 41, No 4, April 1986. pp 445–52

GAUGLER, Barbara B *and* THORNTON, George C. (1989) 'Number of assessment center dimensions as a determinant of assessor accuracy'. *Journal of Applied Psychology.* Vol 74, No 4, August 1989. pp 611–18

GAUGLER, Barbara B *et al.* (1987) 'Meta-analysis of assessment center validity'. *Journal of Applied Psychology*. Vol 72, No 3, 1987. pp 493–511

GLAZE, Tony. (1989) 'Cadbury's dictionary of competence'. *Personnel Management*. Vol 21, No 7, July 1989. pp 44–8.

GOODGE, Peter. (1987) 'Assessment centres: time for deregulation?'. *Management Education and Development*. Vol 18, Part 2, 1987. pp 89–94

GRATTON, Lynda. (1984) 'Assessment centres: the promises and the pitfalls'. Paper presented to the *CRAC Annual Conference*. July 1984

GRATTON, Lynda *and* SYRETT, Michel. (1990) 'Heirs apparent: succession strategies for the future'. *Personnel Management*. Vol 22, No 1, January 1990. pp 34–8

GREATREX, Julian *and* PHILLIPS, Peter. (1989) 'Oiling the wheels of competence'. *Personnel Management*. Vol 21, No 8, August 1989. pp 36–9

GRIFFITHS, Peter *and* ALLEN, Barry. (1987) 'Assessment centres: breaking with tradition'. *Journal of Management Development*. Vol 6, No 1, 1987. pp 18–29

HAGEDORN, Julia. (1989) 'When the best fail the tests'. *Guardian*. 11 April 1989

HERRIOTT, Peter. (1986) 'Assessment centres revisited'. *Guidance and Assessment Review*. Vol 2, No 3, June 1986. pp 7–8

HERRIOTT, Peter. (1988) 'Assessment centres: fashionable fad or flexible friend'. Paper presented to Sectional Meeting 40, *Institute of Personnel Management Conference*, Harrogate, 28 October 1988.

HERRIOTT, Peter. (1989) *Recruitment in the 90s*. London, Institute of Personnel Management, 1989.

HERRIOTT, Peter *et al.* (1985) 'Group decision making in an assessment centre'. *Journal of Occupational Psychology*. Vol 58, 1985. pp 309–12

HORNBY, Derek *and* THOMAS, Raymond. (1989) 'Towards a better standard of management'. *Personnel Management*. Vol 21, No 1, January 1989. pp 52–5

HUCK, James R *and* BRAY, Douglas W. (1976) 'Management assessment center evaluations and subsequent job performance of white and black females'. *Personnel Psychology*, Vol 29, No 1, Spring 1976. pp 13–30

HUNTER, John E *and* SCHMIDT, Frank L. (1983) 'Quantifying the effects of psychological interventions on employee job performance and work-force productivity'. *American Psychologist*. Vol 38, No 4, April 1983. pp 473–8

HUNTER, John E *et al.* (1982) *Metaanalysis: cumulating research findings across studies*. Beverly Hills, Calif, Sage, 1982

ILES, Paul *and* ROBERTSON, Ivan. (1989) 'Unintended consequences and undesired outcomes in managerial selection and assessment'. *Guidance and Assessment Review*. Vol 5, No 3, June 1989. pp 4–5

IMADA, Andrew S *et al.* (1985) 'Applications of assessment centres multinationally: the state of the art, obstacles and cross-cultural implications.' *Journal of Management Development*. Vol 4, No 4, 1985. pp 54–67

JACKSON, Laurence. (1989) 'Turning airport managers into high-fliers'. *Personnel Management*. Vol 21, No 10, October 1989. pp 80–5

JACOBS, Robin. (1989) 'Getting the measure of managerial competence'. *Personnel Management*. Vol 21, No 6, June 1989. pp 32–7

KANTER, Rosabeth Moss. (1989) 'The new managerial work'. *Harvard Business Review*. Vol 89, No 6, November 1989. pp 85–92

KLIMOSKI, Richard *and* BRICKNER, Mary. (1987) 'Why do assessment centers work? The puzzle of assessment center validity'. *Personnel Psychology*, Vol 40, 1987. pp 243–60

KLIMOSKI, Richard *and* STRICKLAND, W J. (1977) 'Assessment centers – valid or merely prescient'. *Personnel Psychology*, Vol 30, 1977. pp 353–61

MABEY, B. (1989) 'The majority of large companies use occupational tests'. *Guidance and Assessment Review*. Vol 5, No 3, June 1989. pp 1–4

MACKINNON, D W. (1977) 'From selecting spies to selecting managers: the OSS assessment program'. In MOSES, J L *and* BYHAM, W C *eds*. *Applying the assessment center method*. New York, Pergamon, 1977

MEGLINO, Bruce M *et al.* (1988) 'Effects of realistic job previews: a comparison using an enhancement and a reduction preview'. *Journal of Applied Psychology*. Vol 73, No 2, 1988. pp 259–66

MEYER, Herbert H. (1987) 'Predicting supervisory ratings versus promotional progress in test validation studies'. *Journal of Applied Psychology*. Vol 72, No 4, 1987. pp 696–7

MISCHEL, Walter. (1968) *Personality and assessment*. New York, Wiley, 1968

MISCHEL, Walter. (1973) 'Toward a cognitive social learning reconceptualization of personality'. *Psychological Review*. Vol 80, No 4, 1973. pp 252–83

NEILL, Arthur. (1989) 'Personal potential'. *Personnel Today*. 30 May 1989. pp 29–33

PEARN, Michael *and* KANDOLA, Rajvinder. (1988)) *Job analysis: a practical guide for managers*. London, Institute of Personnel Management, 1988

PYNES, Joan E *and* BERNARDIN, H John. (1989) 'Predictive validity of an entry-level police officer assessment center'. *Journal of Applied Psychology*. Vol 74, No 5, October 1989. pp 831–3

REDDY, Michael. (1987) *The manager's guide to counselling at work*. Leicester, British Psychological Society, 1987

REILLY, Richard R *and* CHAO, Georgia T. (1982) 'Validity and fairness of some alternative employee selection procedures'. *Personnel Psychology*, Vol 35, 1982. pp 1–62

RITCHIE R J *and* MOSES, J L. (1983) 'Assessment center correlates of women's advancement into middle management: a 7-year longitudinal analysis'. *Journal of Applied Psychology*. Vol 68, 1983. pp 227–31

ROBERTSON, Ivan T. (1985) 'Approaches to the prediction of managerial performance'. Paper presented to the *BPS/ESRC Conference on Managerial Assessment*, UMIST, Manchester, 3 May 1985

ROBERTSON, Ivan T *and* ILES, Paul A. (1988) 'Social representations in assessment centres: candidates' appearance and assessors' judgements'. Paper presented to the *Occupational Psychology Conference of the British Psychological Society*, Manchester, January 1988.

ROBERTSON, Ivan T *and* MAKIN, Peter J. (1986) 'Management selection in Britain: a survey and critique'. *Journal of Occupational Psychology*. Vol 59, 1986. pp 45–57

ROBERTSON, Ivan *et al.* (1987) 'The psychometric properties and design of managerial assessment centres: dimensions into exercises won't go'. *Journal of Occupational Psychology*. Vol 60, No 3, September 1987. pp 187–95

RODGER, David *and* MABEY, Christopher. (1987) 'BT's leap forward from assessment centres'. *Personnel Management*. Vol 19, No 7, July 1987. pp 32–5

ROTHWELL, Sheila. (1985a) 'Manpower matters: the use of assessment centres'. *Journal of General Management*. Vol 10, No 3, Spring 1985. pp 79–84

ROTHWELL, Sheila. (1985b) 'Manpower matters: assessment centre techniques'. *Journal of General Management*. Vol 10, No 4, Summer 1985. pp 91–6

RUSSELL, Craig J. (1985) 'Individual decision processes in an assessment center'. *Journal of Applied Psychology*. Vol 70, No 4, 1985. pp 737–46

RYAN, Ann *and* SACKETT, Paul R. (1989) 'Exploratory study of individual assessment practices: interrater reliability and judgments of assessor effectiveness'. *Journal of Applied Psychology*. Vol 74, No 4, August 1989. pp 568–79

SACKETT, Paul R. (1987) 'Assessment centers and content validity:

some neglected issues'. *Personnel Psychology*, Vol 40, 1987. pp 13–25

SACKETT, Paul R *and* DREHER, George F. (1982) 'Constructs and assessment center dimensions: some troubling empirical findings'. *Journal of Applied Psychology*. Vol 67, No 4, 1982. pp 401–10

SACKETT, Paul R *and* RYAN, Ann M. (1985) 'A review of recent assessment centre research'. *Journal of Management Development*. Vol 4, No 4, 1985. pp 13–27

SCHEIN, Edgar H. (1978) *Career dynamics: matching individual and organizational needs*. Reading, Mass, Addison-Wesley, 1978

SCHMIDT, Frank L *and* HUNTER, John E. (1981) 'Employment testing: old theories and new research findings'. *American Psychologist*. Vol 36, No 10, October 1981. pp 1128–37

SCHMIDT, Frank L *and* HUNTER, John E. (1983) 'Individual differences in productivity: an empirical test of estimates derived from studies of selection procedure utility'. *Journal of Applied Psychology*. Vol 68, No 3, 1983. pp 407–14

SCHMIDT, Frank L *et al.* (1979) 'Impact of valid selection procedures on work-force productivity'. *Journal of Applied Psychology*, Vol 64, No 6, 1979. pp 609–626

SCHMIDT, Frank L *et al.* (1986) 'The economic impact of job selection methods on size, productivity, and payroll costs of the federal work force: an empirically based demonstration'. *Personnel Psychology*. Vol 39, 1986. pp 1–29

SCHMITT, Neal *et al.* (1984) 'Metaanalyses of validity studies published between 1964 and 1982 and the investigation of study characteristics'. *Personnel Psychology*. Vol 37, 1984. pp 407–22.

SCHMITT, Neal *et al.* (1986) 'Changes in self-perceived ability as a function of performance in an assessment centre'. *Journal of Occupational Psychology*. Vol 59, 1986. pp 327–35

SIEGEL, Laurence *and* LANE, Irving M. (1982) *Personnel and organizational psychology*. Homewood, Illinois, Richard D Irwin Inc. 1982

SILVERMAN, William H *et al.* (1986) 'Influence of assessment center methods on assessors' ratings'. *Personnel Psychology*. Vol 39, 1986. pp 565–78

SKAPINKER, Michael. (1989a) 'Playing the game is almost for real'. *Financial Times*. 15 February 1989

SKAPINKER, Michael. (1989b) 'Fast track from the shop floor'. *Financial Times*. 3 July 1989.

SMITH, David *and* TARPEY, Tony. (1987) 'In-tray exercises and assessment centres: the issue of reliability'. *Personnel Review*. Vol 16, No 3, 1987. pp 24–8.

STAMP, Gillian. (1989) 'The individual, the organization, and the path to mutual appreciation'. *Personnel Management*. Vol 21, No 7, July 1989. pp 28–31

STERNBERG, Robert J *and* WAGNER, Richard K *eds.* (1986) *Practical intelligence: nature and origins of competence in the everyday world.* Cambridge, Cambridge University Press, 1986

STEVENS, Christopher. (1985) 'Assessment centres: the British experience'. *Personnel Management*. Vol 17, No 7, July 1985. pp 28–31

STRUBE, Michael J *et al.* (1986) 'Self-evaluation of abilities: accurate self-assessment versus biased self-enhancement'. *Journal of Personality and Social Psychology*. Vol 51, No 1, 1986. pp 16–25

TASK FORCE ON ASSESSMENT CENTER STANDARDS. (1980) 'Standards and ethical considerations for assessment center operations'. *The Personnel Administrator*. Vol 25, 1980. pp 35–8

THERRIEN, M *and* FISCHER, J. (1978) 'Written indicators of empathy: a validation study'. *Counselor Education and Supervision*. Vol 17, 1978. pp 273–7

THORNTON, George C *and* BYHAM W C. (1982) *Assessment centers and managerial performance*. New York, Academic Press, 1982

TREADWELL, David. (1989) 'How Courtaulds find graduates a material factor'. *Personnel Management*. Vol 21, No 11, November 1989. pp 54–5

TURNAGE, Janet J *and* MUCHINSKY, Paul M. (1982) 'Transsituational variability in human performance within assessment centers'. *Organizational Behavior and Human Performance*. Vol 30, 1982. pp 174–200

TURNAGE, Janet J *and* MUCHINSKY, Paul M. (1984) 'A comparison of the predictive validity of assessment center evaluations versus traditional measures in forecasting supervisory job performance: interpretive implications of criterion distortion for the assessment paradigm'. *Journal of Applied Psychology*. Vol 69, No 4, 1984. pp 595–602

WAGNER, Richard K. (1987) 'Tacit knowledge in everyday intelligent behavior'. *Journal of Personality and Social Psychology*. Vol 52, No 6, 1987. pp 1236–47

WALSH, James P *et al.* (1987) 'The effects of gender on assessment centre evaluations'. *Journal of Occupational Psychology*. Vol 60, 1987. pp 305–9

WARMKE, Dennis L. (1985) 'Preselection for assessment centres: some choices and issues to consider'. *Journal of Management Development*. Vol 4, No 4, 1985. pp 28–39

WOOD, Sue *ed.* (1988) *Continuous development: the path to improved performance*. London, Institute of Personnel Management, 1988

WRIGHT, Patrick M *et al.* (1989) 'The structured interview: additional studies and a meta analysis'. *Journal of Occupational Psychology*. Vol 62, Part 3, September 1989. pp 191–9

Author Index

Index